George Fryer

**The Poetry of Various Glees, Songs, &c., as Performed at the Harmonists**

George Fryer

**The Poetry of Various Glees, Songs, &c., as Performed at the Harmonists**

ISBN/EAN: 9783744768177

Printed in Europe, USA, Canada, Australia, Japan

Cover: Foto ©Thomas Meinert / pixelio.de

More available books at **www.hansebooks.com**

# THE
# POETRY

OF VARIOUS

# GLEES, SONGS, &c.

AS PERFORMED AT THE

# Harmonists.

*LONDON:*

Printed at the Philanthropic Reform, London-Road,
St. George's Fields,

## 1798.

# PRESENTED

## TO THE

# 𝔥𝔞𝔯𝔪𝔬𝔫𝔦𝔰𝔱𝔰,

### BY

# *GEORGE FRYER.*

1798.

# INDEX.

## A.

|  | PAGE |
|---|---|
| A ROSE-bud, by Lydia | 20 |
| Amidst the myrtles | 28 |
| A gen'rous friendship | 28 |
| As on a summer's day | 37 |
| As o'er the varied meads | 33 |
| Awake, Æolian lyre | 27 |
| As now the shades of eve | 33 |
| Are the white hours | 70 |
| As I was going to Derby | 76 |
| Away, we've crown'd the day | 71 |
| As passing by a shady grove | 84 |
| Adeste fideles | 86 |
| Ah, why this boding start | 87 |
| Alone, thro' unfrequented wilds | 87 |
| Arise, my sons, prepare for war | 90 |
| Altho' soft sleep | 97 |
| Ask't thou how long | 96 |
| Awake, sweet love | 112 |
| As I saw fair Chlora | 84 |
| A shepherd lov'd a nymph | 100 |
| Amo, amas | 107 |

## B.

| Belinda, see | 7 |
|---|---|
| Blow, blow, thou winter | 19 |
| Blest pair of syrens | 29 |

# INDEX.

|  | PAGE |
|---|---|
| Breathe soft ye winds | 30 |
| Balmy gale | 22 |
| Blow, warder blow | 82 |
| Buz, quoth the blue fly | 104 |
| By the gaily circling glass | 114 |

## C.

|  | |
|---|---|
| Charming to love | 18 |
| Consign'd to dust | 30 |
| Come, shepherds we'll follow | 32 |
| Come, shepherds, come away | 31 |
| Come fairest nymph | 36 |
| Come live with me | 38 |
| Come all noble souls | 34 |
| Canst thou love | 34 |
| Could gold prolong | 35 |
| Cupid, my pleasure | 78 |
| Could a man be secure | 79 |
| Come, oh come, etherial guest | 101 |
| Concord is conquer'd | 108 |
| Come follow me, my lads | 98 |
| Come honest friends | 110 |

## D.

|  | |
|---|---|
| Dear shade of bliss | 9 |
| Discord, dire sister | 32 |
| Do not ask me, charming Phillis | 41 |
| Daughter, sweet of voice | 35 |
| Down, a thousand fathom deep | 88 |
| Ding, ding, ding, dong bell | 107 |

## F.

|  | |
|---|---|
| From Oberon | 11 |
| Fair Phillis I saw | 36 |
| Fill the bowl with rosy wine | 46 |
| Flora gave me fairest flowers | 39 |
| Fair Susan did her wife hode | 40 |
| Fair, sweet, cruel | 43 |

# INDEX.

iii

PAGE

| | |
|---|---|
| Fear no more the heat of the sun | 47 |
| Fair Flora decks | 49 |
| From the fair Lavinian shore | 43 |
| Farewell to Lochaber | 48 |
| Flora now calleth forth | 52 |
| Father of heroes | 77 |
| Flow thou regal purple stream | 91 |
| Fill all the glasses | 92 |

## G.

| | |
|---|---|
| Great Bacchus, O aid us | 40 |
| Gayly I liv'd | 37 |
| Gently touch the warbling | 44 |
| Go, Damon, go | 85 |
| Go, idle boy | 51 |
| Glorious Apollo | 28 |
| Great Apollo strike the lyre | 81 |

## H.

| | |
|---|---|
| How merrily we live | 40 |
| How sleep the brave | 42 |
| Hark, the lark | 45 |
| Here in cool grot | 62 |
| How sweet, how fresh | 44 |
| Hark, the hollow woods | 49 |
| Hence all ye vain delights | 50 |
| How should we mortals | 76 |
| Hey ho, to the greenwood | 108 |
| Halcyon days | 88 |
| Here's a health to all good lasses | 109 |
| Harsh and untuneful | 85 |
| Haste my Nannette | 82 |
| Have you, Sir John Hawkin's | 112 |
| Hark, the bonny Christ Church bells | 106 |

## I.

| | |
|---|---|
| In liquid notes | 7 |
| It was a lover | 12 |

# INDEX.

| | PAGE |
|---|---|
| Jolly Bacchus | 47 |
| In the merry month of May | 53 |
| In paper case | 65 |
| I have been young | 51 |
| In April, when primroses | 72 |
| I lov'd thee beautiful | 21 |
| In a vale clos'd with woodland | 73 |
| I know a bank | 34 |
| It is night, and I am alone | 26 |
| In the sightless air I dwell | 92 |
| I climb the highest clift | 94 |
| If love and all the world | 38 |
| Jack, thou'rt a toper | 92 |
| It was a friar of orders grey | 103 |
| Joan said to John | 114 |
| In verity, damsel | 99 |

## L.

| | |
|---|---|
| Lady, when I behold | 56 |
| Let us, my Lesbia | 50 |
| Lovely seems the moon's | 73 |
| Life's like a ship | 26 |
| Let me careless | 110 |
| Let Rubinelli charm the ear | 105 |
| Lawn as white | 106 |
| Let's drink and let's sing together | 113 |
| Lightly tread | 109 |
| Look, neighbours, look | 94 |

## M.

| | |
|---|---|
| Make haste to meet | 48 |
| Mr. Speaker! though 'tis late | 67 |
| Mark'd you her eye | 25 |
| My mother had a maid | 99 |

# INDEX.

## N.

|   | PAGE |
|---|---|
| Now is the month | 18 |
| Now the bright morning star | 41 |
| Now I'm prepar'd | 68 |
| Non fide al mar | 67 |
| No riches from his scanty | 74 |
| Nor blazing gems | 74 |
| Never till now | 24 |
| Now safe moor'd | 81 |

## O.

| O mistress mine | 14 |
|---|---|
| O sanctissima | 16 |
| O'er William's tomb | 64 |
| Of all the brave birds | 42 |
| O come, O Bella | 63 |
| O, what can equal | 72 |
| O, strike the harp | 30 |
| O thou that rollest | 24 |
| O memory | 93 |
| O happy we | 95 |
| O let the merry peal | 92 |
| O hear a pensive prisoner's | 105 |
| O thou sweet bird | 114 |

## P.

| Pack clouds away | 15 |
|---|---|
| Pretty warbler | 52 |
| Prithee, friend | 45 |
| Peace to the souls | 63 |
| Poculum elevatum | 87 |
| Prithee, foolish boy | 88 |

## R.

| Return blest days | 57 |
|---|---|
| Rise my joy | 65 |

# INDEX.

| | PAGE |
|---|---|
| Return my lovely maid | 52 |
| Round the hapless Andre's | 110 |
| Round with the glass | 112 |

## S.

| | |
|---|---|
| Sober lay and mirthful glee | 5 |
| Shepherds, I have lost | 12 |
| See! o'er the hills | 13 |
| Soft came the breath | 13 |
| Should mirth be observ'd | 14 |
| Sigh no more, ladies | 15 |
| Sister of Phœbus | 46 |
| Sweet muse | 58 |
| Swiftly from the mountain's | 59 |
| Since harmony deigns | 68 |
| Some of my heroes | 23 |
| Since first I saw | 91 |
| Send home my long | 21 |
| Stand to your guns | 102 |
| Sophrosyne, thou guard unseen | 101 |
| Sweet enslaver | 113 |
| Soldier, soldier, take off thy wine | 111 |
| Sweet object of the zephyr's | 108 |
| Sad winter pass'd | 115 |

## T.

| | |
|---|---|
| 'Twas in a village | 6 |
| The waves retreating | 10 |
| Thy form has a resistless | 17 |
| The silver swan | 59 |
| The nightingale, the organ | 59 |
| To me the wanton girls | 61 |
| The mighty conqueror | 66 |
| The fairest flow'rs | 66 |
| Thyrsis, when he left me | 62 |
| The nightingale who tunes | 66 |
| To the old, long life | 97 |
| The cloud cap't towers | 21 |

# INDEX.

| | PAGE |
|---|---|
| The stars of the night arise | 22 |
| Turn, Amarillis | 85 |
| There behold the mighty bowl | 100 |
| Think'st thou, my Damon | 96 |
| To be gazing on those charms | 97 |
| The gods of wit and wine | 102 |
| Then farewell my trim built wherry | 79 |
| To thee, O God | 81 |
| The body of great Elizabeth | 113 |
| To all you Ladies | 98 |
| The storm now subsided | 95 |

## U.

| | |
|---|---|
| Underneath this myrtle shade | 58 |
| Under this stone lies Gabriel John | 115 |

## W.

| | |
|---|---|
| What is love | 8 |
| When Bibo went down | 9 |
| When the toil of day | 16 |
| When gay Bacchus | 69 |
| When all alone | 80 |
| While fools | 68 |
| When Nature form'd | 39 |
| When Sappho | 67 |
| When Arthur first | 61 |
| Welcome sweet pleasure | 54 |
| When for the world's repose | 60 |
| We be soldiers three | 56 |
| When Britain | 55 |
| Where hapless Ilion | 78 |
| What shall he have that kill'd | 69 |
| We be three poor mariners | 57 |
| When winds breathe soft | 60 |
| What Anacreon lov'd | 64 |
| What beauties does Flora | 71 |
| While the moon beams | 70 |
| Who comes so dark | 23 |

# INDEX.

|  | PAGE |
|---|---|
| What shall he have that merits | 25 |
| Wake, sons of Odin | 31 |
| What a frail life | 25 |
| Which is the properest day | 86 |
| Welcome the covert | 109 |
| When Bibo thought fit | 77 |
| When 'tis night | 80 |
| With my jug in one hand | 104 |
| Where the bee sucks | 111 |

## Y.

| Ye spotted snakes | 8 |
|---|---|
| Ye gentle gales | 10 |
| Ye cheerful virgins | 17 |
| Ye British youths | 19 |
| You ask me, dear Jack | 75 |
| You gentlemen of England | 75 |
| You gave me your heart | 65 |

# *POETRY*

## OF VARIOUS

# GLEES, SONGS, &c.

---

HARMONISTS' GLEE.   Three Voices and Chorus.
    Written for this Society by SAMUEL BIRCH.
                                                    *Stevens.*

SOBER lay and mirthful glee,
Harmony, belong to thee!
Thou, with more than chymic art,
From each fibre of the heart
Can'st extract the sigh at will,
And the liquid tear distil:
Or its joyful impulse speak,
Dancing on the dimpled cheek.
Goddess, at this festive hour,
Rich libations will we pour
                  of rosy wine!

### II.

Thou can'st sheath the crimson'd steel,
Bid the soul for others feel;
Cupids, as they wanton round,
In thy fragrant wreaths are bound:
Hymen's torch of hallow'd light
Draws from thee its lustre bright:
Friendship's transports spring from thee,
Sister sweet of Sympathy!
Goddess, at this festive hour,
Rich libations will we pour
                  of rosy wine!

### III.

O descend, angelic maid!
In celestial white array'd,
With tresses fair, which might become
The proudest threads of Pallas' loom,
In thy olive chaplet twin'd,
Flowing gracefully behind.
Sweetly sound thy silver lyre!
Touch the chord! thy sons inspire!
Goddess, at this festive hour,
Rich libations will we pour
    of rosy wine!

---

### BALLAD.

*Dibdin.*

'TWAS in a village, near Castlebury,
 A cobler and his wife did dwell,
And for a time no two so merry,
 Their happiness no tongue cou'd tell.
But to this couple the neighbours tell us
 Did something happen, which caus'd much strife;
For going to a neighbouring alehouse,
 The man got drunk and beat his wife.

### II.

Although he treated her so vilely,
 What did his wife, poor creature do?
Kept snug, and found a method slyly
 To ring his heart quite through and through.
For Dick the tapster, and his master,
 By the report that then was rife,
Were both in hopes, by this disaster,
 To gain the cobler's pretty wife.

### III.

While things went on to rack and ruin,
    And all the furniture was sold;
She seem'd to approve of all was doing,
    And got from each a purse of gold.
So when the cobler's cares were over,
    He vow'd to lead an alter'd life,
To mind his work, ne'er be a rover,
    And love no other than his wife.

---

### GLEE. Four Voices.

ADDISON.               *Stevens.*

BELINDA, see from yonder flowers
    The bee flies loaded to his cell;
Can you perceive what it devours?
    Are they impair'd in shew or smell?

So, tho' I rob you of a kiss
    Sweeter than their ambrosial dew,
Why are you angry at my bliss?
    Has it at all impoverish'd you?

---

### TRIO.

                           *Attwood.*

IN liquid notes,
As music floats;
Listen elves!
'Tis the sound that charms the spheres!
Haste in dew bells, hide yourselves,
Titania appears!

*GLEE.* Four Voices.
BATE DUDLEY.                                    Shield.

WHAT is love? a sad compound of simples most sweet,
Cull'd in life's spring, by fancy, poor mortals to cheat;
A passion no eloquence yet could improve,
So a sigh best expresses the PASSION OF LOVE!

---

*GLEE.* Four Voices.
SHAKSPEARE.                                     Stevens.

YE spotted snakes with double tongue,
Thorny hedgehogs be not seen;
Newts and blind worms do no wrong,
Come not near our fairy queen.
    Philomel with melody,
    Sing in your sweet lullaby,
    Lulla, lulla, lullaby.
    Never harm, nor spell, nor charm,
    Come our lovely lady nigh;
    So good night with lullaby,
    Lulla, lulla, lullaby.

Weaving spiders come not here,
Hence, ye long-legg'd spinners, hence;
Beetles black approach not near,
Worm and snail do no offence.
    Philomel, with melody,
    Sing in your sweet lullaby,
    Lulla, lulla, lullaby.
    Never harm, nor spell, nor charm,
    Come our lovely lady nigh,
    So good night with lullaby,
    Lulla, lulla, lullaby.

## CANZONETTA.

*Mozart.*

DEAR shade of bliss! enchanting hope!
  Thy dreams are almost o'er;
Bewilder'd, weary, faint, I stop,
  My heart believes no more.
Too long my wishes learn'd to stray,
  And truant fancy wander'd far,
To catch a faint and trembling ray,
  From thy obscure and clouded star.

---

## SONG.

*Shroeder.*

WHEN Bibo went down to the regions below,
Where Lethe and Styx in eternity flow;
He awoke, and he cry'd, that he would be row'd back,
That his soul was a dry, and he wanted some sack.
" You were drunk!" replied Charon, " you were drunk
                                        [when you died,
" And you felt not the pain that to death is allied."
" Take me back," roar'd out Bibo, " I mind not the pain,
" Take me back! take me back! let me die once again."

" Forget," replied Charon, " those regions of strife,
" Drink of Lethe divine, 'tis the fountain of life,
" Where the soul is new-born, and the past is a dream,
" And the Gods themselves sip of the care-drowning
                                                     [stream.
" Let the Gods," replied Bibo, " drink water that will,
" The maxims of mortals I'll always fulfil,
" So prate not to me, of your Lethe divine,
" For our Lethe, on earth, is a bumper of wine."

## DUETTO.

*Attwood.*

THE waves retreating from the shore
  In murmurs quit the printless sand;
O'er the green rock the surges pour,
  The white foam lingers on the strand.

We'll search the stores the waters leave,
  Whether of sea-weed, or of shell;
'Till sinking in the western wave,
  The sun's last ray shall bid farewell.

## DUETTO.

*Mozart.*

YE gentle gales that careless blow,
  Regardless of a lover's sighs!
Ye streams unheeding, as ye flow,
  The wretch, who on your margin dies!
Far from your banks we fly to prove
If absence is a cure for love.

Hope not in vain that distant plains,
  Tho' ne'er so fair the flowers they boast;
Or clearer stream can sooth thy pains,
  Or give thee back thy quiet lost:
Ah no! and thou, alas! must prove
That absence is no cure for love.

Hope no more, resolve to fly
  From beauty's tyrant sway;
'Tis nobler in the field to die,
  Than thus to sigh our youth away.

## GLEE.  Four Voices.

BEN JOHNSON.                                              *Stevens.*

FROM Oberon in fairy land,
   The king of ghosts and shadows there,
We fairies all, at his command,
   Are sent to view the night-sports here.
        What revel rout
        Is kept about,
In every corner where we go;
        We will o'er-see,
        And merry be,
And make good sport, with ho, ho, ho!

When lads and lasses merry be,
   With possets and with juncates fine;
Unseen of all the company,
   We eat their cakes and sip their wine;
        O then what sport,
        The wine runs short,
The blushing cheeks with anger glow:
        Their cakes they miss,
        And shriek, who's this?
We answer nought, but ho, ho, ho!

By wells and rills, in meadows green,
   We nightly dance our hey-day guise;
And to our fairy king and queen,
   We chaunt our moon-light minstrelsies.
        Fiends, ghosts, and sprites,
        Who haunt the nights,
The hags and goblins do us know;
        And beldames old
        Our feats have told;
So frolic it, with ho, ho ho!

## GLEE. Four Voices.

SHEPHERDS, I have lost my love,
Have you seen my Anna,
Pride of ev'ry shady grove,
Upon the banks of Banna?
I, for her, my home forsook,
Near yon misty mountain;
Left my flock, my pipe, my crook;
Greenwood shade, and fountain.
Never shall I see them more,
Until her returning;
All the joys of life are o'er,
From gladness chang'd to mourning.
Whither is my charmer flown?
Shepherds, tell me whither!
Ah, woe is me! perhaps she's gone
For ever, and for ever.

---

## GLEE. Five Voices.

SHAKSPEARE. *Stevens. Medal.*

IT was a lover, and his lass,
  With a hey and a ho, and a hey nonino,
That o'er the green corn fields did pass,
  In the spring time;
The pretty spring time, when birds do sing
  Hey ding a ding, sweet lovers love the spring.

And therefore take the present time,
  With a hey and a ho, and a hey nonino;
Now love is crowned with the prime,
  In the spring time;
The pretty spring time, when birds do sing
Hey ding a ding, sweet lovers love the spring.

### GLEE. Three Voices.

*Attwood.*

SEE! o'er the hills the mists retire,
    And stronger grow the beams of day:
Mark! how the flocks wind o'er their brow,
    In vain to shun the scorching ray.
Homeward we trudge—with grateful breast,
And wish our bleeding land at rest!

Merry should the peasant be,
Child of health and labour he!
Nature still with fav'ring smile
Warms his heart and sweetens toil:
Rustic forms and souls of glee,
Merry peasants we will be!

We the purest love can find—
Faithful vows as well as kind:
Lightly then trip life away,
Singing love's sweet roundelay:
Nature wills we should be free
Merry peasants we will be!

---

### SONG. The SHIPWRECK.

Mrs. RATCLIFF.      *Percy.*

SOFT came the breath of spring, smooth flow'd the tide,
    The deck was throng'd, the farewell signs appear,
The anchor weigh'd, the sails expanded wide——
    Mute is each tongue, and eloquent each tear.
The breeze of Eve moans low, her smile is o'er,
    Now sails the vessel t'ward the crimson west:
The sailor youth he climbs the mast once more,
    To see the coast where all his wishes rest.

The storm of midnight swells, the sails are furl'd,
Fast o'er the waves the wretched bark is hurl'd——
Deep sounds the lead; but finds no friendly shore——
" O Ellen! Ellen! we must meet no more!"
Fierce o'er the wreck the whelming waters pass'd,
  The helpless crew sunk in the roaring main:
Henry's faint accents trembled in the blast,
  " Farewell! my love! we ne'er shall meet again!"

---

### GLEE. Five Voices.
SHAKSPEARE. *Stevens.*

O MISTRESS mine! where are you roaming?
O stay and hear, your true love's coming,
  That can sing both high and low;
Trip no further, pretty sweeting,
Journies end in lovers meeting,
  Ev'ry wise man's son doth know.

What is love? 'tis not hereafter,
Present mirth has present laughter;
  What's to come is still unsure:
In delay there lies no plenty,
Then don't leave me, sweet and twenty,
  Youth's a season wont endure.

---

### GLEE. Three Voices.
BATE DUDLEY. *Shield.*

SHOULD mirth be observ'd by her sons to decline,
They recruit her bright lamp with a flask of good wine;
When the glass circles round and our spirits improve,
How sweet flows the bumper to friendship and love.

### GLEE. Five Voices.

SHAKSPEARE.   *Stevens.*

SIGH no more, ladies, sigh no more,
   Men were deceivers ever,
One foot in sea, and one on shore,
   To one thing constant never:

Then sigh not so, but let them go,
   And be you blithe and bonny,
Converting all your sounds of woe
   To hey, nony, nony.

Sing no more ditties, ladies, sing no more,
   Of dumps so dull and heavy;
The frauds of men were ever so,
   Since summer first was leafy:

Then sigh not so, but let them go,
   And be you blithe and bonny,
Converting all your sounds of woe
   To hey, nony, nony.

### GLEE. Five Voices.

HEYWOOD.   *Stevens.*

PACK clouds away, and welcome day,
   With night we banish sorrow;
Sweet air, blow soft, larks, mount aloft,
   To give my love good morrow.
Wings from the wind to please her mind,
   Notes from the lark I'll borrow;
Bird, prune thy wing, nightingale, sing,
   To give my love good morrow;
   Notes from them both I'll borrow.

Wake from thy nest, robin red-breast,
   Sing, birds, in ev'ry furrow :
And from each hill, let music shrill
   Give my fair love good morrow.
Blackbird and thrush, in ev'ry bush,
   Linnet, and cock sparrow ;
You pretty elves, among yourselves,
   To give my love good morrow,
   Sing, birds, in ev'ry furrow.

---

### GLEE. Four Voices.

MERRY.                                *Stevens.*

WHEN the toil of day is o'er,
   And the sheep are in the fold,
And when across the broomy heath
   The whistling winds blow cold ;
When the village dogs, in fear,
   At the moon begin to howl,
And from some tott'ring wall is heard
   The melancholy owl :
Then every danger is abroad,
   And gloomy spectres glide,
While through the air, with dire intent,
   The witch and wizard ride.

---

### *SICILIAN MARINERS' HYMN.* Five Voices and Chorus.

O Sanctissima !
O piissima !
Dulcis Virgo Maria !
Mater amata
Intemerata,
Ora pro nobis.

### GLEE.  Five Voices.

FROM THE PERSIC.                               *Stevens.*

THY form has a resistless grace,
And gladness is thy resting-place;
   Ah, soft enslaver of our minds!
'Tis from thy magic tenderness,
When that fair hand I fondly press,
   That my full heart contentment finds.

Thy coyness, which affects to frown,
Thy dimpled smile, thy cheek of down,
   And the dear mole that on it lies;
Thine eye and eye-brow arch'd so true,
Thy step, majestic to the view,
   All with delight my soul surprize.

---

### GLEE.  Three Voices.

Harmonized by STEVENS.

YE chearful virgins, have you seen
My fair Myrtilla pass the green,
   To rose or jess'mine bow'r?
Where does she seek the woodbine shade?
For sure ye know the blooming maid,
   Sweet as the May-blown flow'r.

Her cheek is like the maiden rose,
Join'd with the lily as it blows,
   Where each in sweetness vie:
Like dew-drops glitt'ring in the morn,
When Phœbus gilds the flow'ring thorn,
   Health sparkles in her eye.

## GLEE.  Five Voices.

Mrs. COWLEY.  *Stevens.*

CHARMING to love is morning's hour,
When from her chrystal roseate tow'r,
She sees the goddess health pursue
The skimming breeze through fields of dew.
Charming the flaming hour of noon,
When the sunk linnet's fading tune
Allures him to the beechy grove;
Or when some cragg'd grotesque alcove,
Sounds in his ear its tinkling rill,
And tempts him to its moss-grown sill.
Most charm'd when on his tranced mind,
Is whisper'd in the passing wind,
The name of her whose name is bliss,
Or when he all unseen can kiss
The fringed bank where late she lay
Hidden from the imperious day.

---

## GLEE.  Five Voices.

*Morley.*

NOW is the month of maying,
When merry lads are playing.
    Fa, la, la, la, la, &c.

Each with his bonny lass,
A dancing on the grass.
    Fa, la, la, la, la, &c.

Leave dulness, care, and sighing,
Remember time is flying.
    Fa, la, la, la, la, &c.

Then quickly haste away,
To keep this holiday.
    Fa, la, la, la, la, &c.

## GLEE. Four Voices.

**Shakspeare.** *Stevens.*

Blow, blow, thou winter wind,
Thou art not so unkind
    As man's ingratitude;
Thy tooth is not so keen,
Because thou art not seen,
    Although thy breath be rude.
Heigh ho! sing heigh ho! unto the green holly,
Most friendship is feigning, most loving meer folly:
    Then heigh ho! the holly, this life is most jolly.

    Freeze, freeze, thou bitter sky,
    Thou dost not bite so nigh
        As benefits forgot:
    Though thou the waters warp,
    Thy sting is not so sharp
        As friend remember'd not.
Heigh ho! sing heigh ho! unto the green holly,
Most friendship is feigning most loving meer folly:
    Then heigh ho! the holly, this life is most jolly.

## SONG.

*Stevens.*

Ye British youths, who danger brave,
When riding on the mountain wave;
Ye guardians of old England's fame,
Assert, assert your country's claim.
    Our tars, so fam'd in story,
        Will sooner die
        Than basely fly,
    And tarnish Britain's glory.

Proud France shall long attempt, in vain,
Upon the azure flood to reign;
She fain wou'd England's birthright seize,
And wield the trident of the seas.
    But tars, so fam'd in story, &c.

This trident is great George's right,
Confirm'd by many a hardy fight;
And they who wrest the same away,
Must fight in blood from day to day.
    For tars, so fam'd in story, &c.

## SONG.

#### The ROSE-BUD.

A ROSE-bud, by Lydia to Emma convey'd,
    Had been wash'd, lately wash'd, by a show'r,
The plentiful moisture encumber'd its head,
    And weigh'd down this beautiful flower.
I hastily seiz'd it, unfit as it was,
    For a nosegay, so drooping and drown'd,
And swinging it rudely, too rudely, alas!
    I snapt it, it fell to the ground.

And such, I exclaim'd, is the pitiless part
    Some act by the delicate mind,
Regardless of wringing and breaking the heart,
    Already to sorrow consign'd.
This delicate rose, had I shaken it less,
    Might have bloom'd with the owner awhile;
Thus the tear that is wip'd with a little address,
    May be follow'd perhaps with a smile.

### GLEE.  Three Voices.

*Stevens.*

SEND home my long-stray'd eyes to me,
Which, oh! too long have dwelt on thee:
But if from you they've learn'd such ill,
  To sweetly smile,
  And then beguile,
Keep the deceivers, keep them still.

Send back my harmless heart again,
Which no unworthy thought could stain:
But if it has been taught by thine,
  To forfeit both
  Its word and oath,
Keep it, for then 'tis none of mine.

### GLEE.  Six Voices.

SHAKSPEARE.          *Stevens.*

THE cloud cap't towers! the gorgeous palaces!
The solemn temples! the great globe itself!
Yea, all which it inherit, shall dissolve!
And like the baseless fabric of a vision,
Leave not a wreck behind!

### ROUND.  Three Voices.

*Battishill.*

I Lov'd thee, beautiful and kind,
And plighted an eternal vow;
So alter'd are thy face and mind,
'Twere perjury to love thee now.

## GLEE Three Voices.

FROM THE PERSIC. *Stevens.*

BALMY gale, I prithee say
   Whence those wings in fragrance dyed?
O'er my love you chanc'd to stray,
   She the perfum'd treat supplied.

Balmy gale, such thefts forbear;
   Other sports from hence pursue;
With the tresses of her hair,
   What have you, O gale, to do?

Yield Narcissus! In her eye
   See what tipsy brightness swims;
There delicious languors lie,
   Drooping grief your lustre dims.

Wisdom! were you left to chuse
   What is sweetest, what is best;
All things else you would refuse,
   If with her you might be blest.

---

## SONG. The GHOST of CARRIL.

OSSIAN. *Percy.*

THE stars of the night arise: they shew their heads of fire, through the flying mist of heaven. But silent and dark is the plain of death! Still on the misty heath arose in my ear the tuneful voice of Carril. He sung of the companions of our youth; and the days of former years; when we met in the hall, and sent round the joy of the shell. The ghosts of those he sung came in the rustling blasts. They were seen to bend t'ward the sound of their praise. O that thou would'st come to my hall when I'm alone by night! And thou dost come, my friend. I hear thy light hand on my harp, when it hangs on the distant wall, and the feeble sound touches my ear. But thou passest away in the murmuring blast; and the winds whistle thro' the grey hairs of Ossian. Thus shall we pass O warriors! like the chiefs of the times of old: for the valiant must one day fall. But the beams of our fame shall rise in the song of victory; and be a light to other days.

*GLEE.* Three Voices.

Ossian. *Callcott.*

WHO comes, so dark, from ocean's roar, like autumn's shadowy cloud? Death is trembling in his hand, his eyes are flames of fire! Son of the cloudy night! retire, call thy winds, and fly: retire thou to thy cave. But let us sit by the mossy fount; let us hear the mournful voice of the breeze, when it sighs on the grass of the cave.

*GLEE.* Five Voices.

Ossian. *Stevens.*

SOME of my heroes are low, I hear the sound of death on the harp. Bid the sorrow rise; that their spirits may fly with joy to Morven's woody hills! Bend forward from your clouds, ghosts of my fathers, bend! bend! bend! Lay by the red terror of your course. Receive the falling chief; whether he comes from a distant land, or rises from the rolling sea. And oh! let his countenance be lovely, that his friends may delight in his presence. Bend forward from your clouds, ghosts of my fathers, bend! bend! bend!

GLEE.  Five Voices.

OSSIAN.                                                    Stevens.

O THOU that rollest above, round as the shield of my fathers! whence are thy beams, O sun? thy everlasting light? Thou comest forth in thy awful beauty; the stars hide themselves in the sky; the moon, cold and pale, sinks in the western wave. But thou thyself movest alone: who can be a companion of thy course? The oaks of the mountains fall: the mountains themselves decay with years: the ocean shrinks and grows again: the moon herself is lost in heaven: but thou art for ever the same; rejoicing in the brightness of thy course. When the world is dark with tempests; when thunder rolls, and lightning flies; thou lookest in thy beauty from the clouds, and laughest at the storm. Thou art, perhaps, like me, for a season; thy years will have an end; thou shalt sleep in thy clouds, careless of the voice of the morning.

---

GLEE.  Four Voices.

Harmonized by HARRISON.

NEVER till now I felt Love's dart,
Guess who it was that stole away my heart,
 'Twas you alone if you'll believe me.

When from this world I'm call'd away,
For you alone I'd wish to stay,
 For you alone if you'll believe me.

'Grave on my tomb when there I'm laid,
" Here lies who lov'd but one dear maid,"
 'Twas you alone if you'll believe me.

( 25 )

### GLEE. Five Voices.

FROM THE ITALIAN. *Stevens.*

WHAT a frail life! in fear and trembling past,
Form'd by a breath, to perish by a blast!
To this sad goal does ev'ry mortal run,
Dust his beginning, and his end a stone.
But yesterday the world in arms he led,
Now in an urn his mouldering dust is laid.

---

### GLEE. Three Voices.

SHERIDAN. *Stevens.*

MARK'D you her eye of heav'nly blue?
Mark'd you her cheek of roseate hue?
That eye in liquid circles moving—
That cheek abash'd at man's approving—
The one love's arrows darting round—
The other blushing at the wound.

---

### ARCHERS' GLEE. Four Voices.

*Stevens.*

WHAT shall he have that merits most,
Who numbers and best shots can boast,
That twang'd the bow with steady eye,
And let the best aim'd arrows fly?
    O, he shall have the bugle horn.

Nor let him think, that in disguise
Some mischief lurks beneath the prize;
For, long before his sire was born,
They often wore a crest of horn.
    Then let him prize the bugle horn.

## SONG.

Ossian. *Percy.*

IT is night, and I am alone, forlorn, on the hill of storms. The wind is heard in the mountain, and the torrent rolls down the rock. No hut receives me from the rain, forlorn, on the hill of the winds.—Rise, O moon, from behind thy clouds, stars of the night appear! lead me some light to the place, where my love rests from the toil of the chace.—His bow near him unstrung, his dogs panting around him. But here must I sit alone, by the rock of the mossy stream; and hear the winds roar; nor can I hear the voice of my love,— no answer, half drown'd in the storm!

---

## SONG.

*Carey.*

LIFE's like a ship, in constant motion,
    Sometimes high and sometimes low;
Where ev'ry one must brave the ocean,
    Whatsoever wind may blow:
If unassail'd by squall or shower,
    Wafted by the gentle gales;
Let's not lose the fav'ring hour,
    While success attends our sails.

Or, if the wayward winds should bluster,
    Let us not give way to fear;
But let us all our patience muster,
    And learn, from Reason, how to steer:
Let judgment keep you ever steady,
    'Tis a ballast never fails;
Should dangers rise, be ever ready
    To manage well the swelling sails.

Trust not too much your own opinion
   While your vessel's under way;
Let good example bear dominion,
   That's a compass will not stray:
When thund'ring tempests make you shudder,
   Or Boreas on the surface rails;
Let good discretion guide the rudder,
   And providence attend the sails.

Then, when you're safe from danger, riding
   In some welcome port or bay;
Hope be the anchor you confide in,
   And care awhile enslumber'd lay:
Or, when each cann's with liquor flowing,
   And good fellowship prevails;
Let each true heart, with rapture glowing,
   Drink "Success unto our sails."

---

### GLEE. Four Voices.

GRAY.                               *Danby. Medal,* 1783.

AWAKE, Æolian Lyre, awake!
   And give to rapture all thy trembling strings;
   From Helicon's harmonious springs,
A thousand rills their mazy progress take.
The laughing flow'rs that round them blow,
Drink life and fragrance as they flow.
Now the rich stream of music winds along,
Deep, majestic, smooth and strong,
Through verdant vales and Ceres' golden reign;
Now rolling down the steep amain,
Headlong impetuous see it pour;
The rocks and nodding groves re-bellow to the roar.

GLEE.  Three Voices and Chorus.

*Webbe.*

GLORIOUS Apollo from on high beheld us,
  Wand'ring to find a temple for his praise,
Sent Polyhymnia hither to shield us,
  While we ourselves such a structure might raise.
    Thus then combining,
    Hands and hearts joining,
  Sing we in harmony Apollo's praise.


Here ev'ry gen'rous sentiment awaking,
  Music inspiring unity and joy;
Each social pleasure giving and partaking,
  Glee and good-humour our hours employ.
    Thus then combining
    Hands and hearts joining,
  Long may continue our unity and joy.


GLEE.  Five Voices.

CAREW.                                          *Battishill.*

AMIDST the myrtles as I walk,
  Love and myself thus enter talk;
Tell me, said I, in deep distress,
Where I may find my shepherdess?


GLEE.  Five Voices.

POPE.                          *Webbe.* Medal, 1768.

A GEN'ROUS friendship no cold medium knows,
  Burns with one love, with one resentment glows:
One should our interest and our passion be,
My friend should hate the man that injures me.

## GLEE. Five Voices.

MILTON.                  Smith. Medal, 1775.

BLEST pair of sirens, pledges of heav'n's joy,
    Sphere-born harmonious sisters, voice and verse,
Wed your divine sounds, and mix'd pow'r employ,
    Dead things with inbreath'd sense able to pierce;
And to our high rais'd phantasy present
That undisturbed song of pure consent,
As sung before the saphire-colour'd throne,
To Him that sits thereon,
    With saintly shout and solemn jubilee;
Where the bright Seraphin in burning row,
Their loud uplifted angel-trumpets blow,
And the cherubic host in thousand quires,
Touch their immortal harps of golden wires,
With those just spirits, that wear victorious palms,
Hymns devout, and holy psalms
    Singing everlastingly:
That we on earth with undiscording voice,
May rightly answer that melodious noise;
As once we did, till disproportioned sin
Jarr'd against nature's chime, and with harsh din
Broke the fair music that all creatures made
To their great Lord, whose love their motion sway'd
In perfect diapason, while they stood
In first obedience, and their state of good.
O! may we soon again renew that song,
And keep in tune with heav'n, till God, ere long,
To his celestial concert us unite,
To live with Him, and sing in endless morn of light.

### GLEE. Three Voices.

PEARCH'S COLLECTION. *Battishill.*

CONSIGN'D to dust, beneath this stone
  In manhood's prime is Damon laid,
Joyless he liv'd but dy'd unknown
  In bleak misfortune's barren shade;
Lov'd by the muse but lov'd in vain,
  'Twas beauty drew his ruin on,
He saw young Daphne on the plain,
  He lov'd, believ'd, and was undone!
Beneath this stone the youth is laid,
  O! greet his ashes with a tear;
May Heav'n with blessings crown his shade,
  And grant that peace he wanted here!

### TRIO.
(With a double accompaniment for the piano forte.)

OSSIAN. *Stevens.*

O STRIKE the harp in praise of my love, the lonely sunbeam of Dunscaith!—Strike the harp in praise of Bragela!—She that I left in the isle of mist, the spouse of Semo's son!—Strike the harp in praise of Bragela!—Lovely with her flowing hair is the white bosom'd daughter of Sorglan!—Strike the harp in praise of Bragela!

### GLEE. Four Voices.

*Webbe.*

BREATHE soft ye winds, ye waters gently flow;
Shield her ye trees, ye flow'rs around her grow;
Ye swains, I beg you pass in silence by,
My love in yonder vale asleep doth lie.

## WAR SONG.

Miss Knipe. *Stevens.*

WAKE, sons of Odin! the returning ray
Will soon arise, and give the promis'd day.
Portents of battle, from the chilly north
Etherial warriors issue swiftly forth;
Their beamy spears and glitt'ring arrows fly
In lambent glory thro' the lucid sky.
The radiant moon drives slow her cloudy car—
Rise, sons of Odin, and prepare for war.

Thrice on my bossy shield I struck my spear,
And thrice a ghost's shrill voice was heard in air;
The sacred oaks that skirt this sloping wood
Are dead—revive their wither'd roots with blood;
The blood of foes shall fertilize the plain,
And Odin's spirit feast on heaps of slain.
Hark! now I hear his mighty voice from far——
Rise, sons of Odin, and prepare for war.

---

### GLEE  Four Voices.

Beaumont and Fletcher. *Lord Mornington.*

COME, shepherds, come away without delay,
While the gentle time doth stay;
Green woods are dumb, and will never tell to any,
Those sweet kisses, and those many
Fond embraces which were giv'n;
Dainty pleasures that could ev'n
In coldest age raise a fire,
And give virgins soft desire;
Come, shepherds, come away without delay,
While the gentle time doth stay.

### GLEE. Four Voices.
CUNNINGHAM. *Dr. Arne.*

COME, shepherds, we'll follow the hearse,
    We'll see our lov'd Corydon laid;
Though sorrow may blemish the verse,
    Yet let the soft tribute be paid.

They call'd him the pride of the plain,
    In sooth he was gentle and kind;
He mark'd in his elegant strain,
    The graces that glow'd in his mind.

No verdure shall cover the vale,
    No bloom on the blossoms appear;
The trees of the forest shall fail,
    And winter discolour the year.

No birds in our hedges shall sing,
    Our hedges so vocal before;
Since he that should welcome the spring,
    Can hail the gay season no more.

### GLEE. Four Voices.
POPE. *Webbe. Medal,* 1772.

DISCORD, dire sister of the slaught'ring pow'r,
Small at her birth, but rising ev'ry hour;
While scarce the skies her horrid head can bound,
She stalks on earth, and shakes the world around.

But lovely Peace, in angel's form,
Descending, quells the rising storm;
Soft Ease and sweet Content shall reign,
And Discord never rise again.

### GLEE. Four Voices.
*Dr. Cooke.*

AS now the shades of eve imbrown
   The scenes where pensive poets rove;
From care remote, from envy's frown,
   The joys of inward calm I prove.
What holy strains around me swell,
   No wildly rude tumultuous sound;
They fix the soul in magic spell,
   Soft let me tread this favour'd ground.
Sweet is the gale that breathes the spring,
   Sweet thro' the vale yon winding stream;
Sweet are the notes loves warblers sing,
   But sweeter friendship's solemn theme.

---

### GLEE. Three Voices.
*Webbe.*

AS o'er the varied meads I stray,
Or trace thro' winding woods my way,
While op'ning flow'rs their sweets exhale,
And odours breathe in ev'ry gale:
Where sage Contentment builds her seat,
And Peace attends the calm retreat;
My soul responsive hails the scene,
Attun'd to joy and peace within.
But, musing on the lib'ral hand
That scatters blessings o'er the land;
That gives for man with pow'r divine,
The earth to teem, the sun to shine;
My grateful heart with rapture burns,
And pleasure to devotion turns.

### GLEE. Four Voices.

*Ravenscroft.*

CAN'ST thou love and live alone, love is so disgraced;
Pleasure is best when it can rest, in a heart embraced.
Rise, rise, day light, do not burn out;
   Bells now ring, and birds do sing,
'Tis only I that mourn out.

Morning star doth now appear,
Wind is hush'd, and sky is clear:
Come away, come, come away,
Can'st thou love? then burn out day.
                        Rise, rise, &c.

### GLEE. Three Voices.

*Dr. Rogers,* 1673.

COME, come all noble souls, who skill'd in music's art,
Do join in this society to bear a part;
For in this pleasant grove we'll sit, we'll drink, and sing,
And imitate those chearful birds now in the spring;
The Muses nine shall know, and all most plainly see,
Our off'ring at their shrine is love and harmony.

### SONG.

*Percy.*

I KNOW a bank whereon the wild thyme blows,
Where oxlips and the nodding violet grows,—
Quite over canopy'd with luscious woodbine,
With sweet musk roses and with eglantine;—
There sleeps Titania, some time of the night,
Lull'd in these flowers with dances and delight.

### GLEE. Three Voices.

ANACREON.                                   *Ireland.*

COULD gold prolong my fleeting breath,
Or guard me from the stroke of death;
Then would I toil for precious ore,
And amass a boundless store.
But since all at length must die!
Nor gold a single hour can buy;
Let the joys of life be mine,
Pour the streams of rosy wine;
Let me taste in Chloe's arms
All the heav'n of beauty's charms;
The smiles of friendship let me prove,
Friendship is the soul of love.

---

### GLEE. Five Voices.

*Webbe.*

DAUGHTER sweet of voice and air,
Gentle Echo, haste thee here;
From the vale, where all around,
Rocks to rocks return the sound:
From the swelling surge that roars
'Gainst the tempest-beaten shores;
From the silent moss-grown cell,
Haunt of warb'ling Philomel:
Where unseen of man you lie,
Queen of woodland harmony.
Daughter sweet of voice and air,
Gentle Echo, haste thee here;
If thou would'st Narcissus move,
To requite thy tender love;
From Delia thou may'st learn the art,
She captivates the hardest heart.

### GLEE. Four Voices.
*Lord Mornington.*

COME, fairest nymph, resume thy reign,
Bring all the graces in thy train;
With balmy breath and flow'ry head,
Rise from thy soft ambrosial bed;
Where, in Elysian slumber bound,
Embow'ring myrtles veil thee round;
Awake, in all thy glories drest,
Recall the zephyr from the west,
Restore the sun, revive the skies,
At nature's call and mine, arise;
Great nature's self upbraids thy stay,
And misses her accustom'd May.
See, all her works demand thy aid,
The labours of Pomona fade;
A plaint is heard from ev'ry tree,
Each budding flow'ret waits for thee.
Come then, with pleasure at thy side,
Diffuse thy vernal spirit wide;
Create, where-e'er thou turn'st thine eye,
Peace, plenty, love, and harmony.

---

### MADRIGAL. Four Voices.
*Morley,* 1596.

FAIR Phillis I saw sitting all alone,
  Feeding her flock, near to the mountain side;
The shepherds knew not whither she was gone,
  But after his lover Amintas hy'd:
Up and down he wander'd while she was missing,
But when he found her, O then they fell a kissing.

## GLEE. Four Voices.

Rowe.                                                 *Smith.*

As on a summer's day,
In a green-wood shade as I lay;
  The maid that I lov'd,
  As her fancy mov'd,
Came walking forth that way:
  And as she passed by
  With a scornful glance of her eye,
    What a shame, quoth she,
    For a swain must it be,
Like a lazy loon for to lie.
And dost thou nothing heed
What Pan our god has decreed?
  What a prize to-day
  Shall be giv'n away
To the sweetest shepherd's reed:
  There's scarce a single swain,
  Of all this fruitful plain,
    But with hopes and fears,
    Now busily prepares
  The bonny boon to gain.
Shall another maiden shine
In brighter array than thine,
  Up, up, dull swain, and make the garland mine.

---

## GLEE. Four Voices.

*Dr. Cooke.*

Gayly I liv'd, as ease and nature taught,
And spent my little life without a thought;
And am amaz'd that Death, that tyrant grim,
Shou'd think of me, who never thought of him.

F

## GLEE. Four Voices.

MARLOWE.                                              Webbe.

COME live with me, and be my love,
And we will all the pleasures prove;
That grove and valley, hill and field,
Or woods and steepy mountains yield.

And I will make thee beds of roses,
And twine a thousand fragrant posies;
A cap of flow'rs, and rural kirtle,
Embroider'd all with leaves of myrtle.

A belt of straw and ivy buds,
A coral clasp and amber studs;
And if these pleasures may thee move,
Then live with me, and be my love.

The shepherd swains shall dance and sing,
For thy delight each May morning;
If joys like these thy mind may move,
Then live with me, and be my love.

---

### ANSWER.

## GLEE. Four Voices.

SIR WALTER RALEIGH.                                   Webbe.

IF love and all the world were young,
And truth in every shepherd's tongue;
Thy fancy'd pleasures might me move,
And I might listen to thy love.

But time drives flocks from field to fold,
Then rivers rage, and hills grow cold ;
Then drooping Philomel is dumb,
And age complains of cares to come.

Thy gowns, thy belts, thy beds of roses,
Thy cap, thy kirtle, and thy posies ;
All these in me can nothing move,
To live with thee, and be thy love.

If youth could last, and love still breed,
Had joys no date, and age no need ;
Then these delights my mind might move,
And I might listen to thy love.

---

### MADRIGAL. Five Voices.

*Wilbye.*

FLORA gave me fairest flowers,
  None so fair in Flora's treasure ;
These I plac'd in Phillis' bowers,
  She was pleas'd, and she's my pleasure :
Smiling meadows seem to say,
Come, ye wantons, here to play.

---

### GLEE. Five Voices.

*Webbe.*

WHEN nature form'd that angel face,
  She lavish'd all her store ;
Be this, she cry'd, my master piece,
  Kneel, mortals, and adore !

*GLEE.*  Five Voices.

*Webbe.*

GREAT Bacchus, O aid us to sing thy great glory,
Thou chief of the gods we assemble before thee:
  Wine's first projector;
  Mankind's protector;
Hail patron of social delights! we adore thee!
All nature rejoic'd when thy birth was declar'd,
Behold here thy altar! and vot'ries prepar'd;
  Crown with thy blessing
  All who confessing,
No pow'r on earth can with thine be compar'd.

---

*GLEE.*  Four Voices.

CHAUCER.          *Dr. Cooke.*

FAIR Susan did her wife hode well maintain,
Algates assaulted so, by lovers twaine;
Now an' I reade arighte that aunciant song,
The paramours were olde, the dame was young:
Had thilk same tale in other guise been told,
Had they been young and she been olde,
Pardie! that wou'd ha' been much sorer tryale,
Full marvailous, I wot, were such denyale.

---

*GLEE.*  Three Voices.

*Este,* 1600.

HOW merrily we live that shepherds be;
Roundelays still we sing with merry glee:
On the pleasant downs, where, as our flocks we see,
We feel no cares, we fear not fortune's frowns.
We have no envy which sweet mirth confounds.
    Da Capo.

### GLEE. Four Voices.

*Webbe.*

Do not ask me, charming Phillis,
  Why I lead you here alone;
By this bank of pinks and lillies,
  And of roses newly blown:
'Tis not to behold the beauty
  Of those flow'rs that crown the spring.
'Tis to!—but I know my duty,
  And dare never name the thing.
'Tis, at worst, but her denying,
  Why should you thus fearful be?
Ev'ry minute gently flying,
  Smiles and says, make use of me.
What the sun does to those roses,
  While the beams play sweetly in;
I wou'd!—but my fear opposes,
  And I dare not name the thing.
Yet I die if I conceal it,
  Ask my eyes, or ask your own;
And if neither can reveal it,
  Think what lovers do alone.
On this bank of pinks and lillies,
  Might I speak what I wou'd do;
I wou'd!—with my lovely Phillis,
  I wou'd—I wou'd!—Ah! wou'd you?

---

### GLEE. Five Voices.

Milton.
*Greville.*

Now the bright morning star, day's harbinger,
Comes dancing from the east, and leads with her
The flow'ry May; who from her green lap throws
The yellow cowslip and the pale primrose.

GLEE.  Four Voices.

COLLINS.                     Dr. Cooke.  Medal, 1771.

How sleep the brave, who sink to rest,
By all their country's wishes blest!
When spring with dewy fingers cold,
Returns to deck their hallow'd mould,
She there shall dress a sweeter sod
Than fancy's feet have ever trod.
By fairy hands their knell is rung,
By forms unseen their dirge is sung,
There honour comes, a pilgrim grey,
To bless the turf that wraps their clay;
And freedom shall awhile repair,
To dwell a weeping hermet there.

---

GLEE.  Three Voices.

*Ravenscroft.*

Of all the brave birds that ever I see,
The owl is the fairest in her degree;
For all the day long she sits in a tree,
And when the night comes, away flies she:
    Te whit, te whoo,
    To whom drink'st thou?
    Sir Noodle, to you!
This song is well sung I make you a vow,
And he is a knave that drinketh now.
    Nose, nose;
And who gave thee that jolly red nose?
    Cinnamon and ginger,
    Nutmeg and cloves,
And they gave me my jolly red nose.

## MADRIGAL. Four Voices.

*Ford.*

FAIR, sweet, cruel, why dost thou fly me?
   O go not from thy dearest,
Tho' thou dost hasten I am nigh thee;
   When thou seem'st far, then I am nearest:
Tarry then and take me with you.

Fie sweetest, here is no danger,
   O fly not, love pursues thee;
I am no foe nor foreign stranger,
   Thy scorn with fresher hope renews me:
Tarry then and take me with you.

## GLEE. Three Voices.

*Dr. Wilson.*

FROM the fair Lavinian shore,
I your markets come to store;
Muse not though so far I dwell,
And my wares come here to sell:
Such is the sacred hunger for gold.
   Then come to my pack,
   While I cry, " What d'ye lack,
What d'ye buy, for here it is to be sold.

I have beauty, honor, grace,
Fortune, favor, time, and place,
And what else thou would'st request,
Ev'n the thing thou likest best:
First let me have but a touch of your gold.
   Then come to me lad,
   Thou shalt have what thy dad
Never gave, for here it is to be sold.

Madam, come, see what you lack,
I've complexions in my pack;
White and red you may have in this place,
To hide your old and wrinkled face.
First let me have but a touch of your gold.
   Then thou shalt seem
   Like a wench of fifteen,
Although you be threescore and ten years old.

---

*GLEE.* Four Voices.

*Paxton. Medal,* 1779.

How sweet, how fresh, this vernal day,
   How musical the air!
Nature was never seen so gay,
   Were but my Silvio near.
Hush! wanton birds, your am'rous song
   Alarms my virgin breast;
Retire, sweet whist'ling winds be gone,
   Retire, 'tis love's request.

---

*GLEE.* Four Voices.

Harmonized from GEMINIANI,

BRADLEY.                       *by Dr. W. Hayes.*

Gently touch the warbling lyre,
   Chloe seems inclined to rest;
Fill her soul with fond desire,
   Softest notes will sooth her breast,
Pleasing dreams assist in love,
Let them all propitious prove.

*GLEE.* Four Voices.

SHAKSPEARE. *Dr. Cooke.*

HARK! the lark at heav'n's gate sings,
    And Phœbus 'gins t'arise,
His steeds to water at those springs,
    On chalic'd flowers that lies.

And winking Marybuds begin
    To ope their golden eyes;
With ev'ry thing that pretty is,
    My lady sweet, arise.

---

*GLEE.* Three Voices.

*Baildon.*

PRITHEE, friend, fill t'other pipe,
    Fie for shame don't let us part;
Just when wit is brisk and ripe,
    Rais'd by wine's all-powerful art.
None but fools would thus retire
    To their drowsy sleepy bed;
Drawer, heap with coals the fire,
    Bring us t'other flask of red.
Foot to foot then let us drink,
    Till things double to our view,
Pleasure then 'twill be to think,
    One full bumper looks like two:
Fill, my friend, then fill your glass,
    Why should we at cares repine?
Misery crowns the sober ass,
    Happiness the man of wine!

### GLEE. Three Voices.

COWLEY'S ANACREON. *Dyne.*

FILL the bowl with rosy wine,
Around our temples roses twine;
And let us chearfully awhile,
Like the wine and roses smile.
To-day is ours, what do we fear?
To-day is ours, we have it here;
Let's treat it kindly, that it may
Wish at least with us to stay:
Let's banish care, let's banish sorrow;
To the gods belongs to-morrow.

---

### GLEE. Five Voices.

MRS. PECKARD. *Webbe.*

SISTER of Phœbus, gentle queen,
Of aspect mild, and ray serene,
Whose friendly beams by night appear,
The lonely traveller to chear!
Attractive power! whose mighty sway
The ocean's swelling waves obey,
And, mounting upward, seem to raise,
A liquid altar to thy praise:
Thee, wither'd hags, at midnight hour,
Invoke to their infernal bow'r:
But I to no such horrid rite,
Sweet queen, implore thy sacred light;
Nor seek, while all but lovers sleep,
To rob the miser's treasur'd heap:
Thy kindly beams alone impart,
To find the youth who stole my heart,
And guide me from thy silver throne,
To steal his heart, or find my own.

### GLEE. Three Voices.

SHAKSPEARE.                                              Dr. Nares.

FEAR no more the heat of the sun,
   Nor the furious winter's rages,
Thou thy worldly task hast done,
   Home art gone to take thy wages;
Golden lads and lasses must
All follow thee, and turn to dust.
No exorciser harm thee!
And no witchcraft charm thee!
Ghost unlaid forbear thee!
Nothing ill come near thee!
Quiet consummation have,
Unremoved be thy grave.

---

### GLEE. Three Voices.

SOMERVILLE.                                              Ireland.

JOLLY Bacchus, hear my pray'r,
Vengeance on th' ungrateful fair;
In thy smiling cordial bowl
Drown all the sorrows of my soul;
Jolly Bacchus! save! oh save!
From the deep devouring grave,
   A poor despairing, sighing swain.

Haste, haste away,
Lash thy tygers, do not stay,
I'm undone if thou delay.
If I view those eyes once more,
I still shall love, and still adore,
And be more wretched than before.

### GLEE. Three Voices.

*Callcott*, M.B.

FAREWELL to Lochaber, and farewell my Jean,
Where heartsome with thee I have many days been;
For Lochaber no more,
May be to return to Lochaber no more.
These tears that I shed, they are all for my dear,
And not for the dangers attending on war;
Tho' borne on rough seas to a far distant shore,
May be to return to Lochaber no more.

---

### GLEE. Four Voices.

*Dr. Arne.*

MAKE haste to meet the gen'rous wine,
Whose piercing is for thee delay'd;
The rosy wreath is ready made, and artful hands prepare
The fragrant oil that shall perfume thy hair.
Fresh roses here with myrtle twine;
  Like Daphne all is fair and sweet,
  But simple all, without deceit,
    My wine from art is free,
  Which never woman was,
    Nor e'er will be.
When nectar sparkles from afar,
  And the free-hearted friend cries, come away,
Make haste, resign thy bus'ness and thy care,
  No mortal int'rest can be worth thy stay.
Here Mirth resides, here Bacchus' rites are due,
Come, drink till ev'ry taper shines like two;
Till whining love in bumpers deep be drown'd,
And all things, like the circling glass, go round.

### GLEE.  Four Voices.

*Smith.*

HARK! the hollow woods resounding,
    Echo to the hunter's cry;
Hark! how all the vales rebounding,
    To his chearing voice reply.
Now so swift o'er hills aspiring,
    He pursues the gay delight;
Distant woods and plains retiring,
    Seem to vanish from his sight.
Flying still, and still pursuing,
    See the fox, the hounds, the men,
Cunning cannot save from ruin;
    Far from refuge, wood, and den.
Now they kill him—homeward hie them,
    For a jovial night's repast;
Thus no sorrow e'er comes nigh them,
    Health continues to the last.

---

### GLEE.  Three Voices.

*Danby.*

FAIR Flora decks the flow'ry ground,
    And plants the bloom of May,
Whilst ev'ry hill, and ev'ry dale,
    Appears unusual gay:
The pretty warblers of the grove
    Assume their various notes;
Th' echoing woods responsive sound,
    The music of their throats.
Lead on, my Celia, quit the town,
    And banish ev'ry care;
O haste, my Celia, haste away,
    To breathe the rural air.

## GLEE. Six Voices.

BEAUMONT and FLETCHER. *Webbe.*

HENCE all ye vain delights!
As short as are the nights
  Wherein you spend your folly!
There's nought in this life sweet,
If man were wise to see't,
  But only Melancholy;
Oh! sweetest Melancholy.

Welcome folded arms and fixed eyes,
A sigh that piercing, mortifies;
A look that's fasten'd to the ground;
A tongue chain'd up—without a sound:

Fountain heads, and pathless groves,
Places which pale passion loves,
Moon-light walks, when all the fowls
Are safely hous'd, save bats and owls.

A midnight bell! a parting groan!
These are the sounds we feed upon!

Then stretch our bones in a still, gloomy valley,
Nothing so dainty sweet as Melancholy.

---

## GLEE. Three Voices.

CATULLUS. *Smith.*

LET us, my Lesbia, live and love,
  Nor cast a moment's thought away;
Whether a peevish world approve,
  Or what they think, or what they say:

The sun that sets shall rise again;
   But when our short-liv'd day is o'er,
One long eternal night must reign,
   A lasting sleep—to wake no more!

Let us then live and love to-day,
And kiss the fleeting hours away.

---

### GLEE. Four Voices.

MERRY.                                  *Callcott*, M.B.

GO, idle boy, I quit thy bow'r,
Thy couch of many a thorn and flow'r,
I wish thee well for pleasures past,
But bless the hour I'm free at last.
Yet still, methinks, the alter'd day
Scatters around a mournful ray;
And chilling ev'ry zephyr blows,
And ev'ry stream untuneful flows;
Haste thee back then, idle boy,
And with thine anguish bring thy joy:
O rend my heart with ev'ry pain,
But let me, let me—love again.

---

### GLEE. Three Voices.

                                               *Dr. Cooke.*

I HAVE been young, though now grown old,
Hardy in field, in battle bold.
I am young still, let who dares try,
I'll conquer or in combat die;
Whatever ye can do or tell,
I one day did you both excell.

### GLEE. Four Voices.

*Hutchinson.*

RETURN, return, my lovely maid,
  For summer's pleasures pass away,
The trees' green liv'ries 'gin to fade,
  And Flora's treasures all decay.
No more, at ev'n-tide, waileth sweet,
  Sad Philomel the woods among;
Nor lark the rising morn doth greet;
  Return, my love, thou stay'st too long.

---

### GLEE. Five Voices.

*Webbe.*

PRETTY warbler, cease to hover,
Pretty warbler, help a lover;
From thy joy a moment borrow,
Tune thy music to my sorrow:
  Join and answer when I mourn.
To grieve alone is most tormenting;
There's a pleasure in lamenting
  My complaint, if you return.

---

### GLEE. Five Voices.

*Smith.*

FLORA now calleth forth each flow'r,
And bids make ready Maia's bow'r,
  Who still doth lie in a trance.
Then will we little love awake,
That now sleepeth in Lethe's lake,
  And pray him leaden our dance.

*GLEE.* Four Voices.

Breton, 1580.  Dr. Cooke. Medal, 1773.

In the merry month of May,
In a morn by break of day,
Forth I walk'd by the wood side,
Where, as May was in his pride,
There I spied all alone
Phillida and Corydon :
Much ado there was, God wot,
For he would love, but she would not ;
She said, never man was true ;
He said, none was false to you ;
He said, he had lov'd her long ;
She said, love should have no wrong :
Corydon would kiss her then ;
She said, maids must kiss no men,
Till they did for good and all :
Then she made the shepherd call
On all the heav'ns to witness truth,
That never lov'd a truer youth.
Thus with many a pretty oath,
Yea and nay, and faith and troth,
Such as silly shepherds use,
When they will not love abuse :
Love, which had been long deluded,
Was with kisses sweet concluded ;
And Phillida, with garland gay,
Was crown'd the Lady of the May.

MADRIGAL.  Five Voices.

*Weelkes.*

WELCOME, sweet pleasure,
My wealth and treasure;
To haste our playing,
There's no delaying,
　　No no no no no!
This mirth delights me,
When sorrow spights me,
Then sing we all, Fa la la;

Sorrow content thee,
Mirth must prevent thee;
Though much thou grievest,
Thou none relievest,
　　No no no no no!
Joy come delight me,
Though sorrow spights me,
Then sing we all, Fa la la.

Grief is disdainful,
Sottish and painful;
Then wait on pleasure,
And lose no leisure,
　　No no no no no!
Heart's ease it lendeth,
And comfort sendeth,
Then sing we all, Fa la la.

*GLEE.* Three Voices.

*Dr. Arne.*

WHEN Britain on her sea-girt shore,
   Her ancient Druids first addrest;
What aid, she cry'd, shall I implore?
   What best defence, by numbers prest?
Tho' hostile nations round thee rise,
   (The mystic Oracles reply'd)
And view thine Isle with envious eyes,
   Their threats defy, their rage deride;
Nor fear invasion from those adverse Gauls,
Britain's best bulwarks are—her wooden walls.

Thine oaks descending to the main,
   With floating force shall stem the tides,
Asserting Britain's liquid reign,
   Where'er thy thund'ring navy rides.
Nor less to peaceful arts inclin'd,
   Where commerce opens all her stores,
In social bands shall league mankind,
   And join the sea-divided shores;
Spread then thy sails where naval glory calls,
Britain's best bulwarks are—her wooden walls.

Hail! happy Isle, what tho' thy vales
   No vine-empurpled tribute yield,
Nor fann'd with odour-breathing gales,
   Nor crops spontaneous glad the field;
Yet Liberty rewards the toil
   Of industry, to labour prone,
Who jocund ploughs the grateful soil,
   And reaps the harvest she has sown:
While other realms tyrannic sway enthralls,
Britain's best bulwarks are—her wooden walls.

## MADRIGAL. Six Voices.

*Wilbye.*

LADY, when I behold the roses sprouting,
   Which clad in damask mantles deck the arbours;
   And then behold your lips, where sweet love harbours,
Mine eyes present me with a double doubting;
For viewing both alike, hardly my mind supposes,
Whether the roses be your lips, or your lips the roses?

---

## GLEE. Three Voices.

*Ravenscroft.*

WE be soldiers three,
   Pardonez moi, je vous en prie;
Lately come forth from the low country,
   With never a penny of money.

Here, good fellow, I drink to thee,
   Pardonez moi, je vous en prie;
To all good fellows wherever they be,
   With never a penny of money.

And he that will not pledge me this,
   Pardonez moi, je vous en prie;
Pays for the shot, whatever it is,
   With never a penny of money.

Charge it again, boy, charge it again,
   Pardonez moi, je vous en prie;
As long as there is any ink in my pen,
   With never a penny of money.

### GLEE. Four Voices.

**Dr. Percy.**            *Smith.*

RETURN, blest days, return ye laughing hours,
   Which led me up the roseate steep of youth,
Which strew'd my simple path with vernal flow'rs,
   And bid me court chaste science and fair truth.
Witness ye winged daughters of the year,
   If e'er a sigh had learnt to heave my breast,
If e'er my cheek was conscious of a tear,
   Till Cynthia came, and robb'd my soul of rest.
So soft, so delicate, so sweet she came,
   Youth's damask glow just dawning on her cheek;
I gaz'd, I sigh'd, I caught the tender flame,
   Felt the fond pang, and droop'd with passion weak.

---

### GLEE. Three Voices.
*Ravenscroft.* 1614.

WE be three poor mariners,
   Newly come from the seas,
We spend our lives in jeopardy,
   While others live at ease:
Shall we go dance the round, around, around,
   And he that is a bully, boy,
     Come pledge me on this ground.
We care not for those martial men,
   That do our states disdain,
But we care for those merchantmen,
   Which do our states maintain;
To them we dance this round, around, around,
   And he that is a bully, boy,
     Come pledge me on this ground.

### GLEE. Four Voices.

ANACREON.                                                    *Dr. Arne.*

SWEET Muse! inspire thy suppliant bard,
Heroic ardor to record.
In vain the fervent pray'r I move,
Hark! ev'ry echo whispers Love!
I'll raise the theme to acts renown'd——
Ah! no,—'tis Love,—no other sound!
Farewell then, Patriot—Hero—King!
My Muse of nought but Love can sing.

---

### GLEE. Three Voices.

COWLEY.                                                   *Battishill.*

UNDERNEATH this myrtle shade,
On flow'ry beds supinely laid,
With od'rous oils my head o'erflowing,
And around it roses growing,
What should I do but drink away
The heat and troubles of the day?
In this more than kingly state,
Love, himself, shall on me wait.
Fill to me, love, nay fill it up;
And mingled, cast into the cup
Wit, and mirth, and noble fires,
Vig'rous health, and gay desires.
Crown me with roses whilst I live,
Now your wines and ointments give;
After death I nothing crave,
Let me alive my pleasures have,
All are stoicks in the grave.

### GLEE.  Four Voices

CUNNINGHAM.  *Webbe.*

SWIFTLY from the mountain's brow,
   Shadows nurs'd by night retire,
And the peeping sun-beams now
   Paint with gold the village spire.

Sweet, O sweet, the warbling throng
   On the white emblossom'd spray,
Nature's universal song
   Echoes to the rising day.

---

### GLEE.  Three Voices.

*Weelkes.*

THE nightingale, the organ of delight,
   The nimble lark, the blackbird, and the thrush,
And all the pretty choristers of flight,
   That chaunt their music notes on ev'ry bush:
Let them no more contend who shall excel;
The cuckow is the bird that bears the bell.

---

### GLEE.  Five Voices.

*Gibbons.*

THE silver swan who living had no note,
When death approach'd unlock'd her silent throat:
Leaning her breast against the reedy shore,
Thus sung her first and last, and sung no more:
Farewell all joys, O death, come close mine eyes,
More geese than swans now live, more fools than wise.

### GLEE. Five Voices.

*Webbe.*

WHEN winds breathe soft along the silent deep,
The waters curl, the peaceful billows sleep:
A stronger gale the troubled wave awakes;
The surface roughens, and the ocean shakes.
More dreadful still, when furious storms arise,
The mounting billows bellow to the skies;
On liquid rocks the tott'ring vessel's toss'd,
Unnumber'd surges lash the foaming coast:
The raging waves, excited by the blast,
Whiten with wrath, and split the sturdy mast,
When in an instant, he who rules the floods,
Earth, air, and fire, Jehovah, God of gods,
In pleasing accents speaks his sovereign will,
And bids the waters, and the winds, be still!
Hush'd are the winds, the waters cease to roar;
Safe are the seas, and silent as the shore.
Now say what joy elates the sailor's breast,
With prosp'rous gales so unexpected blest:
What ease, what transport, in each face is seen,
The heav'ns look bright, the air and sea serene:
For ev'ry plaint we hear a joyful strain
To Him, whose pow'r unbounded rules the main.

### GLEE. Four Voices.

*Earl of Mornington.*

WHEN for the world's repose my fairest sleeps,
   See Cupid hovers round her couch and weeps;
Well may'st thou weep, proud boy, thy power dies,
   Thou hast no dart when Chloe has no eyes.

### GLEE. Three Voices.

*Callcott*, M.B.

WHEN Arthur first in court began,
   To wear long hanging sleeves,
He entertain'd three serving men,
   And all of them were thieves.

The first he was an Irishman,
   The second was a Scot,
The third he was a Welchman,
   And all were knaves I wot.

The Irishman lov'd Usquebaugh,
   The Scot lov'd ale, call'd Blue Cap;
The Welchman, he lov'd toasted Cheese,
   And made his mouth like a mouse trap.

Usquebaugh burnt the Irishman,
   The Scot was drown'd in ale;
The Welchman had like to be choak'd with a mouse,
   But he pull'd her out by the tail.

---

### GLEE Three Voices.

ANACREON.                                               *Webbe*.

TO me the wanton girls insulting say,
Here in this glass thy fading bloom survey.
Just on the verge of life, 'tis equal quite,
Whether my locks are black, or silver white;
Roses around my fragrant brows I'll twine,
And dissipate anxieties in wine.

## GLEE. Four Voices.

SHENSTONE.                                *Lord Mornington.*

HERE in cool grot and mossy cell
We rural fays and fairies dwell;
Tho' rarely seen by mortal eye,
When the pale moon ascending high,
Darts thro' yon limes her quiv'ring beams,
We frisk it near these crystal streams;
Her beams reflected from the wave,
Afford the light our revels crave;
The turf with daisies 'broider'd o'er,
Exceeds, we wot, the Parian floor;
Nor yet for artful strains we call,
But listen to the water-fall.

---

## GLEE. Four Voices.

GRAY.                                      *Callcott,* M.B.

THYRSIS when he left me swore,
   In the spring he would return;
Ah! what means that op'ning flow'r,
   And the bud that decks the thorn?
'Twas the nightingale that sung,
'Twas the lark that upward sprung.

Idle notes, untimely green,
   Why such unavailing haste?
Gentle gales and skies serene,
   Prove not always winter past;
Cease my doubts, my fears to move;
Spare the honour of my love.

### GLEE. Three Voices.

OSSIAN.  *Callcott,* M.B.

PEACE to the souls of the heroes,
Their deeds were great in fight;
Let them ride around me on clouds,
Let them shew their features in war;
My soul then shall be firm in danger,
And mine arm like the thunder of heav'n:
But be thou on a moon-beam, O Morna,
Near the window of my rest,
When my thoughts are of peace,
When the din of arms is past.

---

### GLEE. Three Voices.

ROLLI.  *Webbe.*

O COME O bella l'ardor de vini,
   Piu coralini tuoi la-bri fa,
Bacco vi stilla, suave umore,
   D'un tal sapore che amor non ha,
Bevil' O cara, quando ha la spuma,
   Tal si costuma gustarlo qui,
Cosi gridando l'ama il francese,
   Cheto l'Inglese l'ama cosi.
Ma cara luci voi non vedete,
   Qual altra siete sui l'abri sta,
Aita il core ch' è tutto fuoco,
   Et a poco a poco mancando va.
Si bella Dori godiam che il giorno,
   Presto è al ritorno presto al partir,
Di giovanezza godiam il fiore,
   Poi l'ultim' ore lasciam venir.

### GLEE   Three Voices.

FAWKES.                                                            Baildon.

WHAT Anacreon lov'd we drink,
   Press it closely to the lip;
Misers, can ye sleep or think,
   While such nectar here we sip?


Our gay honest Horace would take off his flask,
   While Ovid in love play'd the fool:
Come, broach the Falernian or Massic old cask,
   And follow gay Horace's rule.


Let the whining lover sigh,
   All his tears are shed in vain;
But a bumper can supply,
   Ev'ry tear that love can drain.


Love was ne'er a treasure,
Drinking is a pleasure,
   Then fill your gen'rous goblet high!
Let your glasses gingle
Thus our joys we mingle,
   Drink, sons of Bacchus, till ye die.

---

### GLEE.   Four Voices.

Norris, M.B.

O'ER William's tomb, with silent grief opprest,
Britannia mourns her hero now at rest;
Not tears alone, but praises too she gives,
Due to the guardian of our laws and lives:
Nor shall that laurel ever fade with years,
Whose leaves are water'd with a nation's tears.

### GLEE.  Four Voices.
*Webbe.*

RISE, my joy, sweet mirth attend,
I'm resolv'd to be thy friend;
Sneaking Phœbus hides his head,
He's with Thetis gone to bed:
Tho' he will not on me shine,
Still there's brightness in the wine;
From Bacchus I'll such lustre borrow,
My face shall be a sun to-morrow.

---

### GLEE.  Four Voices.
*Dr. Cooke.*

IN paper case, hard by this place,
   Dead a poor dormouse lies;
And soon or late, summon'd by fate,
   Each prince, each monarch dies.

Ye sons of verse, while we rehearse,
   Attend instructive rhime;
No sins had Dor to answer for,—
   Repent of your's in time.

---

### GLEE.  Five Voices.
CRADDOCK                *Webbe. Medal,* 1776.

YOU gave me your heart t'other day,
   I thought it as safe as my own;
I've not lost it,—but, what can I say?
   Not your heart from mine can be known!

### GLEE. Four Voices.

*Webbe.*

THE mighty conqueror of hearts,
  His pow'r I here deny;
With all his flames, his fires and darts,
I, champion-like, defy.

I'll offer all my sacrifice,
  Henceforth, at Bacchus' shrine;
The merry god ne'er tells us lies,
  There's no deceit in wine.

---

### GLEE. Three Voices.

*Danby. Medal,* 1788.

THE fairest flow'rs the vale prefer,
And shed ambrosial sweetness there;
While the tall pine and mountain oak,
Oft feel the tempest's ruder stroke:
So in the lowly moss-grown seat,
  Dear peace and quiet dwell;
The storms that rack the rich and great,
  Fly o'er the shepherd's cell.

---

### GLEE. Four Voices.

*Danby.*

THE nightingale who tunes her warbling notes so sweet,
'Midst flowers ne'er presumes to fix her mournful seat;
Melodiously she sings, while hawthorns pierce her breast,
Her voice sweet echo rings, and nature lulls to rest.

### GLEE. Three Voices.

Metastasio. Webbe. Medal.

Non fide al mar che freme,
  La temeraria prora,
Chi si scolora e teme,
  Sol quando vede il mar:
Non si cimenti in Campo,
Chi trema al suono e al lampo;
D'una guerriera tromba
D'un bellicoso acciar.

### GLEE. Three Voices.

Smollett. Danby. Medal, 1781.

When Sappho tun'd the raptur'd strain,
The list'ning wretch forgot his pain;
With art divine, the lyre she strung,
Like thee she play'd, like thee she sung.
For when she struck the quiv'ring wire,
The eager breast was all on fire;
But when she tun'd the vocal lay,
The captive soul was charm'd away.

### CATCH. Three Voices.

Lord Sandwich. Baildon.

Mr. Speaker! though 'tis late,
I must lengthen the debate.
Question—Order—hear him, hear!
Pray support, support the chair!
Sir, I shall name you if you stir.

### GLEE. Four Voices.

*Webbe.*

NOW I'm prepar'd to meet th' enchanting scene,
This is the hour the happy guests convene;
Welcome this kind release from care,
What can to social joys compare?
With wine and songs the jovial night shall pass,
Till morning darts its rays into my glass;
When vine-crown'd Bacchus leads the way,
What can his votaries dismay?

---

### GLEE. Four Voices.

*Smith. Medal, 1776.*

WHILE fools their time in stormy strife employ,
Be ours engag'd in Union, Peace and Joy;
Thus the blest gods, the genial day prolong
In feasts ambrosial, and celestial song;
Apollo tunes the lyre, the muses round,
With voice alternate, aid the silver sound.
} Pope's Iliad.
Wisely we imitate the Pow'rs divine,
Peace at our heart, and pleasure our design.

---

### GLEE. Four Voices.

*Webbe.*

SINCE harmony deigns with her vot'ries to dwell,
Exalt ev'ry voice, and each note loudly swell;
Intreat her to visit us here ev'ry night,
And thus by her presence diffuse new delight;
And since she such mirth and such pleasure can bring,
Let us Io Pæan repeatedly sing.

### GLEE. Four Voices.

SHAKSPEARE.                      *Smith.*

WHAT shall he have that kill'd the deer?
His leathern skin and horns to wear;
The horn, the horn, the lusty horn,
Is not a thing to laugh to scorn.

Take you no scorn to wear the horn,
It was a crest ere thou wert born;
Thy father's father wore it,
And thy father bore it:

The horn, the horn, the lusty horn,
Is not a thing to laugh to scorn.

---

### GLEE. Three Voices.

ANACREON.             *Baildon. Medal,* 1766.

WHEN gay Bacchus fills my breast,
All my cares are lull'd to rest;
Rich I seem as Lydia's king,
Merry catch, or ballad sing:
Ivy wreaths my temples shade,
Ivy, that will never fade;
Thus I sit in mind elate,
Laughing at the farce of state;
Some delight in fighting fields,
Nobler transports Bacchus yields;
Fill the bowl, I ever said,
'Tis better to lie drunk than dead.

## GLEE. Four Voices.

ANNUAL REGISTER.          *Callcott*, M.B.

ARE the white hours for ever fled,
  That us'd to make the cheerful day?
And ev'ry blooming pleasure dead,
  That led th' enraptur'd soul astray?
Too fast the rosy-footed train,
  The blest delicious moments past:
Pleasure must now give way to pain,
  And grief succeed to joy at last.
O! daughters of eternal Jove,
  Return with the returning year;
Bring pleasure back, and smiles, and love,
  Let blooming love again appear.

---

## GLEE. Three Voices.

RANNIE.          *Callcott*, M.B.

WHILE the moon-beams, all bright,
Give a lustre to night,
  I'll weep on his dwelling so narrow,
And high o'er his grave,
The willow trees wave,
  Who died on the banks of the Yarrow.

'Twas under this shade,
Hand in hand as we stray'd,
  He fell by the flight of an arrow;
And fast from the wound,
His blood stain'd the ground,
  Who died on the banks of the Yarrow.

## TWEED-SIDE. Four Voices.

### Harmonized by CORFE.

WHAT beauties does Flora disclose!
  How sweet are her smiles upon Tweed!
Yet Mary still sweeter than those,
  Both nature and fancy exceed.
No daisy nor sweet blushing rose,
  Nor all the gay flow'rs of the field
Not Tweed gliding gently thro' those,
  Such beauty and pleasure does yield.

'Tis she does the virgins excel,
  No beauty with her may compare;
Love's graces all round her do dwell,
  She's fairest where thousands are fair.
Say, charmer, where do thy flocks stray?
  Oh! tell me at noon where they feed?
Shall I seek them on sweet winding Tay,
  Or the pleasanter banks of the Tweed?

---

## GLEE. Three Voices.

*Webbe.*

AWAY! away! we've crown'd the day,
  The hounds are waiting for their prey:
The huntsman's call invites ye all,
  Come in, boys, while ye may.

The jolly horn, the rosy morn,
  With harmony of deep-mouth'd hounds:
For these, my boys, are sportsman's joys,
  Our pleasure knows no bounds.

## GLEE. Three Voices.

REID. *Webbe.*

O! what can equal here below,
  The life of us three brothers!
The rising sigh of bursting woe,
  The balm of friendship smothers.
The stream of life so smoothly flows,
  We scarcely feel it gliding;
No dang'rous wave the current knows,
  Our bark with harm betiding:
Nor anxious thought, nor teasing care,
  Our peace of mind destroying;
The social glass we freely share,
  Thus doubly life enjoying.
In friendship's ties so firmly bound,
  Misfortune's storms we weather,
And ev'ry blast that would confound,
  Unites us more together.

---

## GLEE. Four Voices.

### YELLOW-HAIR'D LADDIE.

#### Harmonized by CORFE.

IN April, when primroses paint the sweet plain,
And summer approaching rejoiceth the swain,
The yellow-hair'd laddie would often-times go,
To wilds and deep glens, where the hawthorn trees grow:

There, under the shade of an old sacred thorn,
With freedom he sung his love ev'ning and morn;
He sung with so soft and enchanting a sound,
That silvans and fairies unseen danc'd around.

## ELEGY. Three Voices.

*Jackson.*

IN a vale clos'd with woodland, where grottoes abound,
Where rivulets murmur, and echoes resound;
I vow'd to the muses my time and my care,
Since neither could win me the smiles of my fair.

As freedom inspir'd me, I rang'd and I sung,
And Daphne's dear name never fell from my tongue;
But if a smooth accent delighted my ear,
I could wish unawares that my Daphne might hear,

With fairest ideas my bosom I stor'd,
To drive from my heart the fair nymph I ador'd!
But the more I with study my fancy refin'd,
The deeper impression she made on my mind.

Ah! whilst I the beauties of nature pursue,
I still must my Daphne's fair image renew;
The graces have chosen with Daphne to rove,
And the muses are all in alliance with love!

---

## GLEE. Four Voices.

MOORISH BALLAD.           *Callcott,* M.B.

LOVELY seems the moon's fair lustre
    To the lost benighted swain,
When all silv'ry bright she rises,
    Gilding mountain, grove, and plain.
Lovely seems the sun's full glory
    To the fainting seaman's eyes,
When some horrid storm dispersing,
    O'er the wave his radiance flies.

### GLEE. Four Voices.

*Danby.*

NOR blazing gems, nor silken sheen,
Bespeak the wearer's heart serene;
Nor purple robe, nor tissued vest,
Proclaim the calm unruffled breast.
The crimson mantle, and the jewell'd crown,
Fair peace forsakes, well pleas'd to own
The shepherd's simple garb and russet gown.
Sweet peace forsakes the crouded street,
And shelters in the calm retreat;
With solitude the charmer dwells,
'Midst rural meads and flow'ry dells:
She shuns the costly feast, and rare,
Contented with the shepherd's fare;
She scorns the roofs where nobles dwell,
And seeks the rustic's humbler cell;
She slights the miser's glitt'ring hoard,
The joys of wine, and plenteous board;
Fair virtues livery she wears,
And all the joys of life are hers.

---

### GLEE. Four Voices.

Miss WILLIAMS.                                 *R. Cooke.*

NO riches from his scanty store
   My lover could impart;
He gave a boon I valu'd more,
   He gave me all his heart.
But now for me, in search of gain,
   From shore to shore he flies;
Why wander riches to obtain,
   When love is all I prize!

GLEE.  Three Voices.

*Dr. Arne.*

YOU ask me, dear Jack, for an emblem that's rife,
And clearly explains the true medium of life:
I think I have hit it, as sure as a gun,
A bowl of good punch and the medium are one.
When lemon and sugar so happily meet,
The acid's corrected by mixing the sweet;
The water and spirit so luckily blend,
That each from th' extreme doth the other defend.
Then fill up the bowl, rot sorrow and strife,
A bumper! my boys, to the medium of life:
Which keeps our frail state in a temper that's meet,
Contented in blending the sour with the sweet.

---

GLEE.  Three Voices.

OLD BALLAD. *Callcott*, M.B.

YOU, gentlemen of England, that live at home at ease,
Ah! little do you think upon the dangers of the seas;
Give ear unto the mariners, and they will plainly show,
All the cares and the fears, when the stormy winds do blow.

If enemies oppose us, when England is at wars
With any foreign nations, we fear not wounds nor scars,
Our roaring guns shall teach 'em our valour for to know,
Whilst they reel on the keel, when the stormy winds do blow.

Then, courage all brave mariners, and never be dismay'd,
Whilst we have bold adventurers we ne'er shall want a trade;
Our merchants will employ us to fetch them wealth we know,
Then be bold, work for gold, when the stormy winds do blow.

## GLEE. Three Voices.

OLD BALLAD. *Callcott,* M.B.

As I was going to Derby,
  'Twas on a market-day,
I met the finest ram, Sir,
  That ever was fed upon hay;
This ram was fat behind, Sir,
  This ram was fat before,
This ram was ten yards high, Sir,
  Indeed, he was no more!

The butcher that kill'd this ram, Sir,
  Was up to his knees in blood!
The boy that held the pail, Sir,
  Was carried away by the flood!
The tail that grew upon his rump
  Was ten yards and an ell,
And that was sent to Derby,
  To toll the market bell.

---

## GLEE. Three Voices.

BATE DUDLEY. *Sacchini.*

How should we mortals spend our hours?
  In war, in love, and drinking!
None but a fool consumes his pow'rs
  In peace, in care, and thinking.

Time, would you let him wisely pass,
  Is lively, brisk and jolly:
Dip but his wing in the sparkling glass,
  And he'll drown dull melancholy.

### GLEE. Five Voices.

Ossian. *Callcott*, m.b.

FATHER of heroes! high dweller of eddying winds,
    Where the dark-red thunder marks the troubled clouds;
    Open thou thy stormy halls;
    Let the bards of old be near.
We sit at the rock, but there is no voice;
    No light but the meteor of fire.
    O! from the rock on the hill,
    From the top of the windy steep,
    O! speak, ye ghosts of the dead!
    O! whither are ye gone to rest?
In what cave of the hill shall we find the departed?
    No feeble voice is on the gale;
    No answer half-drown'd in the storm!
Father of heroes! the people bend before thee;
Thou turnest the battle in the field of the brave;
    Thy terrors pour the blasts of death!
    Thy tempests are before thy face!
    But thy dwelling is calm, above the clouds;
    The fields of thy rest are pleasant.

---

### DUETTO.

*Travers.*

WHEN Bibo thought fit from the world to retreat,
As full of champaign as an egg's full of meat;
He wak'd in the boat, and to Charon he said
" He would be row'd back, for he was not yet dead?"
" Trim the boat and sit quiet," stern Charon replied,
" You may have forgot, you were drunk when you died."

( 78 )

### GLEE.  Four Voices.

Dr. Aikin.  *Webbe.*

WHERE, hapless Ilion, are thy heav'n-built walls,
Thy high embattled tow'rs, thy spacious halls?
Where are thy temples, fill'd with forms divine?
Where is thy Pallas? where her awful shrine?
The mighty Hector where? thy fav'rite boast;
And all thy valiant sons, a splendid host?
Thy arts, thy arms, thy riches, and thy state,
Thy pride, thy pomp, thy all that made thee great?
These prostrate now in dust and ruin lie,
But thy transcendant fame can never die;
Fate boasts no pow'r to sink thy glories past,
They fill the world, and with the world shall last.

---

### GLEE.  Four Voices.

#### Lovers and Bacchanals.

*Webbe.*

**Lovers.**
CUPID, my pleasure, soft love I thee implore;
**Bacchanals.**
Bacchus, my treasure, brisk wine I will adore:
**Lovers.**
Give me a beautiful maid to bless my longing arms!
**Bacchanals.**
Give me a bumper of red, in that I view all charms.
**Lovers.**
Without thy joy, life soon would cloy,
   And prove a mere disease;
**Bacchanals.**
The noble juice will mirth produce,
   And give us ease.          Da Capo.

## DUETTO.

*Goodwin.*

COULD a man be secure,
That his life would endure,
As of old, for a thousand long year;
What arts might he know,
What acts might he do,
And all without hurry or care.

But we that have but span long lives,
The thicker must lay on the pleasure;
And since time will not stay,
We'll add the night unto the day;
And thus we'll fill the measure.

## SONG.

*Dibdin.*

THEN farewell my trim built wherry,
Oars, and coat and badge farewell;
Never more at Chelsea ferry,
Shall your Thomas take a spell.

But to hope and peace a stranger,
In the battles heat I go;
Where expos'd to ev'ry danger,
Some friendly ball may lay me low.

Then may hap when homeward steering,
With the news my mess-mates come;
Even you, my story hearing,
With a sigh may cry poor Tom.

## SONG.

SHERIDAN.                                              Linley.

WHEN 'tis night, and the mid-watch is come,
And chilling mists hang o'er the dark'ned main;
Then sailors think of their far distant home,
And of those friends they ne'er may see again;
But when the fights begun,
Each serving at his gun,
Shou'd any thought of them, come o'er your mind:
Think only should the day be won;
How 'twill cheer,
Their hearts to hear,
That their old companion he was one.

Or, my lad, if you a mistress kind,
Have left on shore, some pretty girl and true,
Who many a night doth listen to the wind,
And sighs, to think how it may fare with you:
O when the fights begun,
Your serving at your gun,
Should any thought of her come o'er your mind:
Think only should the day be won;
How 'twill cheer,
Her heart to hear
That her own true sailor he was one.

*MADRIGAL.* Five Voices.
*Converso.* 1580.

WHEN all alone my pretty love was playing,
And I saw at a gaze, bright Phœbus staying,
Alas! I fear'd there would be some betraying.

## GLEE. Four Voices.

*Webbe.*

GREAT Apollo, strike the lyre,
Fill the raptur'd soul with fire!
Let the festive song go round,
Let this night with joy be crown'd.
Hark! what numbers soft and clear,
Steal upon the ravish'd ear!
Sure, no mortal sweeps the strings;
Listen!—'tis Apollo sings!

## SONG.

NOW safe moor'd with bowl before us,
Mess-mates heave a hand with me;
Lend a brother sailor chorus,
While he sings your lives at sea.

O'er the wide waves swelling ocean,
Toss'd a loft or hurl'd below;
As to fear, 'tis all a notion,
When our time's come we must go.
     Da Capo.

## SONG.

Louis the Sixteenth's Appeal and Resignation.

*Maynard.*

TO thee, O God, I make my last appeal;
To all the world, my innocence reveal;
Forgive my enemies, by whom I die,
Through zeal misled, or cruel perfidy.

## DUETTO.

*Travers.*

HASTE my Nannette, my lovely maid,
Haste to the bow'r, thy swain has made;
For thee alone, I've made the bow'r,
And strew'd the couch, with many a flow'r.
None but my sheep shall near us come,
Venus be prais'd, my sheep are dumb;
Great god of love, take thou my crook,
To keep the wolf from Nannettes flock.
Guard thou the sheep, to her so dear,
My own alas! have left my care;
But of the wolf if thou'rt afraid,
Come not to us to call for aid.
For with her swain, my love shall stay;
Tho' the wolf strole, and the sheep stray.

---

## GLEE. Three Voices.

*Callcott,* M.B.

BLOW warder, blow thy sounding horn,
And thy banner wave on high;
For the Christians have fought in the holy land,
And have won the victory.
Loud the warder blew his horn,
And his banner wav'd on high;
Let the mass be sung,
And the bells be rung,
And the feast eat merrily.
The warder look'd from the tow'r on high,
As far as he could see,
I see a bold knight, and by his red cross,
He comes from the east country.

Then loud the warder blew his horn,
And call'd till he was hoarse,
I see a bold knight,
And on his shield bright,
He beareth a flaming cross.
Then down the lord of the castle came,
The red cross knight to meet,
And when the red cross knight he espied
Right loving he did him greet.
Thour't welcome here, dear red cross knight,
For thy fame's well known to me,
And the mass shall be sung,
And the bells shall be rung,
And we'll feast right merrily.
Oh, I am come from the holy land,
Where saints did live and die;
Behold the device I bear on my shield,
The red cross knight am I:
And we have fought, in the holy land,
And we've won the victory,
For with valiant might,
Did the Christians fight,
And made the proud Pagans fly:
Thour't welcome here, dear red cross knight,
Come lay thy armour by,
And for the good tidings thou dost bring,
We'll feast us merrily.
For all in my castle shall rejoice,
That we've won the victory;
And the mass shall be sung,
And the bells shall be rung,
And the feast eat merrily.

## DUETTO.

*Hayden.*

As I saw fair Chlora walk alone,
The feather'd snow, came softly down:
As Jove descending from his tow'r,
To court her in a silver show'r.
The wanton snow flew to her breast,
As little birds into their nest;
But being o'ercome with whiteness there,
For grief dissolv'd into a tear.
Thence falling on her garments hem,
To deck her froze into a gem.
The wanton snow, &c.
    Da Capo.

---

## GLEE.   Five Voices.

*Danby.*

As passing by a shady grove,
 I heard a linnet sing,
Whose sweetly plaintive voice of love
 Proclaim'd the cheerful spring.
His pretty accents seem'd to flow
 As if he knew no pain;
His downy throat he tun'd so sweet,
 It echo'd o'er the plain.
Ah! happy warbler, I reply'd,
 Contented thus to be;
'Tis only harmony and love
 Can be compar'd with thee.

### GLEE.  Three Voices.

*Brewer,* 1667.

TURN, Amarillis, to thy swain,
Thy Damon calls thee back again;
Here's a pretty arbour by,
Where Apollo cannot spy;
Here let's sit, and whilst I play,
Sing to my pipe a roundelay.

---

### ANSWER.

### GLEE.  Four Voices.

*Paxton.*

GO, Damon, go, Amarillis bids adieu,
Go seek another love,
But prove to her more true:
No, no, I care not
For your pretty arbour nigh,
Although great Apollo cannot spy:
Nor will I sit to hear you play,
Nor tune my voice to your roundelay.

---

### SONG.

STERNE.

HARSH and untuneful are the notes of love,
Unless my Julia strikes the key:
Her hand alone can touch the part
Whose dulcet movement charms the heart,
And governs all the man, with sympathetic sway.
O Julia!

## GLEE. Four Voices.

*Dr. Arne.*

WHICH is the properest day to drink,
Saturday, Sunday, Monday?
Each is the properest day I think,
Why should I name but one day?
Tell me but yours, I'll mention my day,
Let us but fix on some day.
Tuesday, Wednesday, Thursday, Friday,
Saturday, Sunday, Monday.

---

## PORTUGUESE HYMN. Five Voices.

ADESTE, fideles, læti triumphantes,
Venite, venite in Bethlehem;
Natum videte regem angelorum,
Venite, adoremus Dominum.

Deum de Deo Lumen de Lumine,
Gestant puella viscera;
Deum verum genitum non factum,
Venite, adoremus Dominum.

Ergo, qui natus die hodierna,
Jesu, tibi sit gloria;
Patris æterni verbum caro factum,
Venite, adoremus Dominum.

Cantet nunc Io! chorus angelorum,
Cantet nunc aula cœlestium;
Gloria in excelsis Deo!
Venite, adoremus Dominum.

## GLEE. Four Voices.

CAWTHORNE.     ABELARD.     *J. W. Callcott.*

AH, why this boding start, this sudden pain,
That wings my pulse, and shoots from vein to vein?
What mean regardless of yon midnight bell,
These earth-born visions, saddening o'er my cell:
What strange disorder prompts these thoughts to glow,
These sighs to murmur and these tears to flow!
Sleep, conscience, sleep, each awful thought be drown'd,
And seven-fold darkness veil the scene around.
What means this pause, this agonizing start,
This glimpse of heav'n just rushing through my heart?
Methinks I see a radiant cross display'd,
A wounded Saviour bleeds along the shade:
Around th'expiring God, bright angels fly,
Swell the loud hymn, and open all the sky.
O save me! save me! ere the thunder roll
And endless terrors swallow up my soul.
Fly! for justice bares the arm of God,
And the grasp'd vengeance only waits His nod!

---

## GLEE. Five Voices.

*W. Rock.*

ALONE thro' unfrequented wilds,
With pensive steps I rove;
I ask the rocks, I ask the streams,
Where dwells my absent love.
The silent eve, the rosy morn,
My constant search survey;
But who can tell if thou my dear,
Wilt e'er remember me?

( 88 )

### GLEE.  Three Voices.

*Stevens.*

PRITHEE, foolish boy, give o'er,
Cease thy bosom to torment;
Prithee, sigh and whine no more,
Come with me and taste content;
Love's a foe of thine and mine,
Let's drown the god in gen'rous wine.

---

### GLEE.  Four Voices.

*Dr. Cooke.*

HALCYON days, now wars are ending,
You shall find whene'er you sail,
Tritons all the while attending
With a kind and gentle gale;
No stars again shall hurt you from above,
But all your days shall pass in peace and love.

                     Da Capo.

---

### SONG.

Mrs. RATCLIFF.                                                    *Percy.*

DOWN, down, a thousand fathom deep,
Among the sounding seas I go,
Play round the foot of ev'ry steep,
Whose cliffs above the ocean grow,
In coral bow'rs I love to lie
And hear the surges roll above,
And thro' the waters view on high,
The proud ship's sail and gay clouds move:

And oft at midnight's stillest hour,
When summer seas the vessel lave,
I love to prove my charmful pow'r
While floating on the moon-light wave;
And when deep sleep the crew has bound,
And the sad lover musing leans
O'er the ship's side, I breathe around,
Such strains as speak no mortal means.

Sometimes a single note I swell,
That softly sweet at distance dies;
Then wake the magic of my shell,
When choral voices round me rise,
The trembling youth charm'd by my strain,
Calls up the crew who silent bend,
O'er the high deck, but list in vain,
My song is hush'd, my wonders end.

---

### GLEE. Five Voices.

*Dr. Arne.*

POCULUM elevatum,
Quod nobis est pergratum;
Poculum elevatissimum,
Quod nobis est pergratissimum;
Bibamus!
Bibe, totum extra,
Nil manet intra;
Hoc est bonum in visceribus meis,
Hoc est bonum in visceribus tuis;
Et nos con sequimur laudes tuas.
O Quam bonum est!
O Quam jocundum est!
Poculis fraternis gaudere.

## DUETTO.

*Eccles.*

FILL all the glasses, fill them high,
Drink and defy all pow'r but Love;
Wine gives the slave his liberty,
But Love makes a slave of thundring Jove.
Then drink, drink away,
Make a night of the day,
'Tis nectar, 'tis liquor divine;
The pleasures of life,
Free from anguish and strife,
Are owing to Love, and good wine.

## AMERICAN INDIAN WAR SONG.

*Percy.*

ARISE, my sons, prepare for war,
The spirit calls us hence afar:
By moon-ey'd night, or sunny day,
Thro' marsh and forest speed your way;
Nor heat, nor cold, nor hunger fear,
The Indian ev'ry pain can bear,
When strangers of the morning shore,
Forget the oaths their fathers swore.

Arise, arise, prepare, 'tis day,
The spirit calls us hence away:
With printless foot, the foe surprise,
Or close in death his sleeping eyes:
With wily war and patient toil,
We'll feast us on revenge and spoil:
Then strangers of the morning shore,
Shall keep the oaths their fathers swore.

## SONG.

*Dr. Arnold.*

FLOW, thou regal purple stream,
Tincted by the solar beam:
In my goblet sparkling rise,
Cheer my heart, and glad my eyes.
My brain ascend on Fancy's wing,
'Noint me, Wine, a jovial king:
While I live, I'll lave my clay,
When I'm dead, and gone away;
Let my thirsty subjects say,
A month he reign'd, but that was May.

---

## GLEE. Four Voices.

*Ford,* 1620.

SINCE first I saw your face I resolv'd
To honour and renown you;
If now I be disdain'd, I wish
My heart had never known you:
What I that lov'd, and you that lik'd,
Shall we begin to wrangle?
No, no, no! my heart is fast,
And cannot disentangle.

The sun whose beams most glorious are,
Rejecteth no beholder,
And your sweet beauty past compare,
Made my poor eyes the bolder.
Where beauty moves, and wit delights,
And signs of kindness bind me;
There, O there, where-e'er I go,
I'll leave my heart behind me.

*CATCH.* Three Voices.

*Danby.*

O LET the merry peal go on,
Proclaim how happy Jane's with John:
With lasses gay and lads elate,
The loves and graces round them wait;
Of Jane and John shall be my song,
Of Jane and John the whole day long.

---

*CATCH.* Three Voices.

*Purcell.*

JACK, thou'rt a toper, let's have t'other quart,
Ring, we're so sober 'twere a shame to part,
None but a cuckold bully'd by his wife,
For coming late fears a domestick strife;
I'm free, so are you, to call and knock,
Knock boldly, the watchman cries past two o'clock.

---

*SONG.*

Mrs. Radcliff.

*Percy.*

IN the sightless air I dwell;
On the sloping sun beams play,
Delve the cavern's inmost cell,
Where never yet did day-light stay;
Dive beneath the green sea waves,
And sport amid the briny deep,
Skim ev'ry shore that Neptune laves,
From Lapland's plain to India's steep.

And listen to celestial sounds
That swell the air unhear'd of men,
As I watch my nightly rounds
O'er woody steep and silent glen;
Then when the breeze has sunk away,
And ocean scarce is heard to lave,
For me the sea nymphs softly play,
Their dulcet shells beneath the wave.

In thrilling sounds that murmur woe,
And pausing silence makes more dread,
In music, breathing from below,
Sad solemn sounds that wake the dead,
Unseen I move, unknown am fear'd,
And Fancy's wildest dreams I weave,
And oft by bards my voice is heard,
To die along the gales of Eve.

---

### GLEE. Four Voices.

SHENSTONE. *Stevens.*

O MEMORY! celestial maid!
Who gleans't the flowrets cropt by time,
And suff'ring not a leaf to fade,
Preserv'st the blossoms of our prime!
Bring, bring those moments to my mind,
When life was new, and Lesbia kind.
And bring that garland to my sight,
With which my favor'd crook she bound;
And bring that wreath of roses bright
Which then my festive temples crown'd:
And to my raptur'd ear convey,
The gentle things she deign'd to say.

## SONG.

### LAMENTATION OF ABBA THULE.

*Percy.*

I CLIMB the highest clift, I hear the sound
Of dashing waves, I gaze intent around,
But not a speck can my long straining eye,
A speck or shadow o'er the waves descry,
That I might weep tears of delight and say,
It is the bark that bore my child away.
Oft in my silent cave when to its fire
From the night's rushing tempest we retire,
Methought the wild waves said amid the roar
At midnight—Thou shalt see thy son no more.
Is he cast bleeding on some desert plain?
Upon his father does he call in vain?
Oh, I shall never, never hear his voice:
The spring-time shall return, the isles rejoice;
But faint and weary I shall meet the morn,
And 'mid the cheering sunshine droop forlorn;
The joyous conch sounds in the high wood loud;
O'er all the beach now stream the busy croud,
And light canoes along the lucid tide,
With painted shells and sparkling paddles glide:
I linger on the desert rock alone,
Heartless? and cry for thee, my son! my son!

---

### CATCH. Three Voices.

*Harrington.*

LOOK, neighbours, look! here lies poor Thomas Day,
   Dead, and turn'd to clay.
Does he, sure? what old Thomas? lackaday!
     Poor soul! no, no; aye, aye, aye, aye, aye.

## GLEE.  Three Voices.

*Callcott*, M.B.

OH! happy we,
Attune to harmony,
That with heart, hand and voice,
Thus united rejoice:
Say, does the star from heav'n dropping,
Or the wind the pale rose cropping,
Figure right the quick decline
Of thy heart's friendship unto mine.

Ah, no! no! no!
As violets blow,
Still fresh, and still pure
Shall our friendship endure;
Nor shall the star from heav'n dropping,
Or the wind, the pale rose cropping,
Figure right the quick decline
Of thy heart's friendship unto mine.

## DUETTO.

*Attwood.*

THE storm now subsided, with pleasure we view
Those waves that derided the pray'rs of the crew;
Again behold, they're now serene,
'Tis thus in life's uncertain scene,
   Da Capo.

Now rescu'd from danger, on England's blest shore,
Thou home of the stranger, we greet thee once more;
To all, yet to thy sons most dear,
Who breathe, but must thy air revere.
   Da Capo.

### GLEE. Four Voices.

SHERIDAN. *Stevens.*

ASK'T thou, how long my love shall stay
When all that's new is past?
How long? Ah! Delia, can I say
How long my life will last?
Dry be that tear, be hush'd that sigh,
At least I'll love thee till I die.

And does that thought affect thee too;
The thought of Damon's death,
That he who only lives for you
Must yield his faithful breath:
Hush'd be that sigh, be dry that tear,
Nor let us lose our heaven here.

---

### ANSWER.

### GLEE. Four Voices.

*Stevens.*

THINKS'T thou, my Damon, I'd forego
This tender luxury of woe;
Which better than the tongue imparts
The feelings of impassion'd hearts:
Blest if my sighs and tears but prove
The winds and waves that waft to love.

Can true affection cease to fear,
Poor is the joy not worth a tear:
Did passion ever know content,
How weak the rapture words can paint:
Then let my sighs and tears but prove
The winds and waves that waft to love.

### GLEE. Five Voices.

**Carey.**                                                            *Stevens.*

TO be gazing on those charms,
To enfold thee in these arms,
From those lips to hear thy vow,
With extatic sweetness flow ;
To be lov'd by one so fair
Is to be blest beyond compare.

At that bosom's gentle shrine,
To confess what glows in mine ;
In those heav'nly eyes to view,
That confession dear to you ;
To be lov'd by one so fair
Is to be blest beyond compare.

### CATCH. Three Voices.

                                                                       *Webbe.*

TO the old, long life and treasure ;
To the young, all health and pleasure ;
   To the fair, their face
   With eternal grace,
And the rest to be lov'd at leisure.

### GLEE. Five Voices.

                                                                       *Stevens.*

ALTHO' soft sleep death's near resemblance wears,
Still do I wish him on my couch to lie :
Come, balmy rest, for sweetly it appears,
Thus without life to live, thus without death to die.

### GLEE. Three Voices.

EARL OF DORSET. *Callcott*, M.B.

To all you ladies now at land,
    We men at sea indite;
But first would have you understand,
    How hard it is to write:
The Muses now, and Neptune too,
We must implore to write to you.
    With a fal, lal, lal, lal, la.

In justice you cannot refuse,
    To think of our distress;
When we, for hopes of honor, lose
    Our certain happiness.
All these designs are but to prove
Ourselves more worthy of your love.
    With a fal, lal, lal, lal, la.

And now we've told you all our loves,
    And likewise all our fears;
In hopes this declaration moves
    Some pity for our tears:
Let's hear of no inconstancy,
We have enough of that at sea.
    With a fal, lal, lal, lal, la.

---

### CATCH. Three Voices.

*Warren.*

Come follow me, my lads, let's merry be;
Ding, ding, dong bell, let's merry be;
Now, now, I follow thee, let's merry be.

## SONG.

*Dibdin.*

IN verity, damsel, thou surely wilt find
   That my manners are simple and plain,
That my words and my actions, my lips and my mind,
   By my own good will never are twain;
I love thee, would move thee,
   Of love to be partaker.
Relent then, consent then,
   And take thy upright Quaker.

Tho' vain I am not, nor of fopp'ry possest,
   Would thou yield to be wedded to me,
Thou would'st find, gentle damsel, a heart in my breast,
   As joyful, as joyful could be;
I love thee, would move thee,
   Of love to be partaker.
Relent then, consent then,
And take thy upright Quaker.

---

## GLEE. Four Voices.

SHAKSPEARE.                                          *Shield.*

MY mother had a maid call'd Barbara;
She was in love, and he she lov'd prov'd false,
And did forsake her.
She had a song of Willow, an old song 'twas;
But it express'd her fortune, and she died
Singing it.—That song to night will not
Go from my mind; I've much ado, not to
Go hang my head all a'one side,
And sing it like poor Barbara.

## GLEE. Three Voices.

A SHEPHERD lov'd a nymph so fair, fal, la, la, la.
And thus his passion did declare, fal, la, la, la.
For thee, dear maid, I long in vain,
Have sigh'd, nor ventur'd to complain,
O now consent to ease my pain.
     Fal, la, la, la.

O could I gain thy tender heart, fal, la, la, la.
We'd join again no more to part, fal, la, la, la.
With thee I'd tread the daisied mead,
To view the herds and flocks at feed,
And home at eve thy footsteps lead.
     Fal, la, la, la.

With blushing sweetness thus the maid, fal, la, la, la.
His honest passion brief repaid, fal, la, la, la.
I long, dear youth, thy love have known,
By ev'ry tender kindness shewn,
Then take my hand, my heart's thy own.
     Fal, la, la, la.

---

## DUETTO.
*Webbe.*

THERE, behold the mighty bowl!
Now I'll quench my thirsty soul:
Richest fragrance flows around,
All our cares shall here be drown'd.
Hail, great Bacchus! pow'r divine,
These, and such like gifts are thine;
Of thy praise our song shall be,
While we thus are blest by thee.

GLEE.  Four Voices.

Dr. Scott.                                         Paxton.

COME, oh come, etherial guest!
   Child of tranquil ease and pleasure;
Ever blessing, ever blest,
   Here diffuse thy choicest treasure.
Come, sweet Mirth, and bring with thee,
Sportive catch, and merry glee;
But ah, sly nymph, all playful tricks remove,
   Let no offensive sounds invade the ear,
But such as bashful Beauty may approve,
   And Modesty, without a blush, can hear.
Then this blooming radiant throng,
   Shall applaud the festive measures;
Darting heav'nly smiles along,
   Giving and receiving pleasures:
What sweet raptures fire the mind,
When beauty's charms, and music are combin'd!

———

GLEE.  Five Voices.

Hayley.                                           Dr. Cooke.

SOPHROSYNE, thou guard unseen,
   Whose delicate controul
Can turn the discord of chagrin
   To harmony of soul.
Above the lyre, the lute above,
   Be mine thy melting tone,
Which makes the peace of all we love,
   The basis of our own.

O

## SONG.

*Carter.*

STAND to your guns my hearts of oak,
Let not a word on board be spoke,
Victory soon will crown the joke,
   Be silent and be ready.
Ram home your guns, and spunge them well,
Let us be sure the balls will tell,
The cannons roar shall sound their knell,
   Be steady, boys, be steady.
Not yet ; reserve your fire,
I do desire.——Fire.
Now the elements do rattle,
The gods amaz'd behold the battle,
   A broadside, my boys.
See the blood in purple tide,
Trickle down her batter'd side,
Wing'd with fate the bullets fly,
Conquer, boys, or bravely die.
Hurl destruction on your foes.
   She sinks! Huzza!
To the bottom down she goes.

---

## GLEE. Four Voices.

*Webbe.*

THE gods of wit and wine, and love prepare,
With chearful bowls to celebrate the fair ;
Love is enjoin'd to name his fav'rite toast,
We'll give, " The goddess, that delights us most ;"
Phœbus appoints, and bids the trumpet sound,
And Bacchus in a bumper puts it round.

( 103 )

## GLEE. Three Voices.

SHAKSPEARE. *Callcott*. M.B.

IT was a friar, of orders grey,
  Went forth to tell his beads ;
And he met with a lady fair,
  Clad in a pilgrim's weeds.
Now heav'n thee save, thou holy friar,
  I pray thee tell to me,
If ever at yon holy shrine,
  My true love thou didst see ?
" And how should I know your true love,
  " From many another one ?"
" O by his cockle hat and staff,
  " And by his sandal shoone."
" O, lady! he's dead and gone,
  " And at his head a green grass turf,
" And at his heels a stone.
  " Weep no more lady,
  " Thy sorrow is in vain,
" For violets pluckt, the sweetest show'rs
  " Will ne'er make grow again :
" Yet stay, fair lady, rest awhile,
  " Beneath yon cloister wall,
" See, through the hawthorn blows the cold wind,
  " And drizzly rain doth fall."
" O stay me not, thou holy friar,
  " O stay me not, I pray ;
" No drizzly rain that falls on me,
  " Can wash my fault away."

## GLEE. Three Voices.

*Smart.*

WITH my jug in one hand, and my pipe in the other,
I drink to my neighbour and friend;
All my cares in a whiff, of tobacco I smother,
For life I know shortly must end.
While Ceres most kindly refills my brown jug,
   With good ale I will make myself mellow;
In my old wicker chair I will seat myself snug,
   Like a jolly and true happy fellow.

I'll ne'er trouble my head with the cares of the nation,
   I've enough of my own for to mind;
The cares of this life are but grief and vexation,
   To death we must all be consign'd:
Then I'll laugh, drink and sing, and leave nothing to pay,
   But drop like a pear that is mellow;
And when cold in my coffin, I'll leave them to say,
   He's gone like a hearty good fellow.

## CATCH. Four Voices.

BEN JOHNSON. *Dr. Arne.*

BUZ, quoth the blue fly; hum, quoth the bee;
Buz and hum they cry, and so do we;
In his ear, in his nose, thus do you see:
He eat the dormouse, else it was he.

## DUETTO

Dr. Wake.            Dr. Cooke.

LET Rubinelli charm the ear,
  And sing as erst with voice divine;
To Carbonelli I adhere,
  Instead of music give me wine.
And yet, perhaps, with wine combin'd,
  Sweet music wou'd our joys improve;
Let both together then be join'd,
  And feast we as the gods above!
Anacreon like, we'll sit and quaff,
  Old age and wrinkles I'll despise;
Devote the present hours to laugh,
  And learn to-morrow to be wise.

---

## GLEE. Four Voices.

Mrs. Barbauld.            Dr. Cooke.

O HEAR a pensive prisoner's pray'r, for liberty who sighs,
And never let thy heart be shut against a wretches cries;
If e'er thy breast with freedom glow'd, and spurn'd a tyrant's
                                                    [chain,
Let not thy strong oppressive force, a free-born mouse
                                                    [detain.
So may thy hospitable board with health and peace be crown'd,
And every charm of heart-felt ease, beneath thy roof be
                                                    [found;
So when destruction lurks unseen, which men like mice
                                                    [may share,
May some kind angel clear thy path, and break the hidden
                                                    [snare.

GLEE. Three Voices.

SHAKSPEARE.                               Dr. Cooke.

LAWN as white as driven snow,
Cyprus black as e'er was crow ;
Gloves as sweet as damask roses,
Masks for faces, and for noses.
Bugle bracelets, necklace amber,
Perfume for a lady's chamber ;
Golden coifs and stomachers
For my lads to give their dears.
Pins, and shining toys of steel,
What maids lack from head to heel ;
Come, buy of me, buy lads, buy,
Come buy, or else your lasses cry.

---

ROUND. Three Voices.

Dr. Aldrick.

HARK! the bonny Christ-church bells,
One, two, three, four, five, fix,
  They sound so woundy great,
  So wondrous sweet,
  And they troul so merrily.
Hark! the first and second bell,
That ev'ry day at four and ten
Cries, come, come, come, come, come to pray'rs,
And the verger troops before the dean.
Tingle, tingle, ting, goes the small bell at nine,
To call the beerers home ;
But there's ne'er a man will leave his can,
'Till he hears the mighty Tom.

## ROUND, Four Voices.

*Stoner.*

DING, ding, ding dong bell,
O cruel death, that stopp'd the breath
　Of him I lov'd so well:
Alack and well aday, 'tis a heavy day,
　That ever us befell;
Then for his sake, some order let us take,
　That we may ring his knell.

---

## GLEE. Three Voices.

AMO, amas, I love a lass,
As a cedar tall and slender,
Sweet cowslips grace,
Is her nominative case,
And she's of the feminine gender.
　　Rorum, corum, sunt divorum,
　　Harum, scarum, divo:
　　Tag, rag, merry, derry,
　　Perriwig and hatband;
　　Hic, hoc, horum, genetivo.

Can I decline a nymph divine,
Her voice like a flute is dulcis;
Her occulus bright, her manus white,
And soft when I tacto her pulse is.
　　　　Rorum. Da Capo.

O, how bella my Puella,
I'll kiss secula seculorum;
If I've luck, sir, she's my uxor,
O dies benedictorum.　Rorum. Da Capo.

CANON.  Three Voices.

HEY ho, to the greenwood now let us go,
Sing heave and ho;
And there shall we find both buck and doe,
Sing heave and ho;
The hart and hind and the little pretty roe,
Sing heave and ho.

GLEE.  Five Voices.
R. Cooke.

CONCORD is conquer'd! in this urn their lies,
The master of great music's mysteries;
And in it is a riddle, like the cause,
Will Lawes* was slain by those whose wills were laws.

GLEE.  Three Voices.
Lord Mornington.

SWEET object of the zephyr's kiss,
Come Rose, come courted to my bow'r:
Queen of the banks, the garden's bliss,
Come and abash yon tawdry flow'r.
Why call us to revokeless doom,
With grief the op'ning buds reply,
Not suffer'd to extend our bloom;
Scarce born, alas! before we die.
Man having past appointed years,
Ours are but days, the scene must close,
And when fate's messenger appears,
What is he but a wither'd rose.

\* Musician to Charles I. killed at the siege of West Chester.

### GLEE. Three Voices.

LIGHTLY tread, 'tis hallow'd ground,   *Scotland.*
Hark, above, below, around,
Fairy bands their vigils keep,
While frail mortals sink to sleep,
And the moon with feeble rays,
Gilds the brook that bubbling plays;
As in murmurs soft it flows,
Music sweet for lovers' woes.

### GLEE. Three Voices.

WELCOME the covert of these aged oaks,   *Mellish.*
Welcome each cavern of these horrid rocks,
Far from the world's illusion let me rove,
Deceiv'd in friendship, and betray'd in love.

### GLEE. Three Voices.

HERE'S a health to all good lasses,   *Guglielmi.*
Pledge it merrily, fill your glasses,
   Let a bumper toast go round;
May they live a life of pleasure,
Without mixture without measure,
   For with them true joys are found.

### GLEE  Four Voices.
*Paxton.*

ROUND the hapless Andre's urn
Be the cyprus foliage spread;
Fragrant spice profusely burn,
Honors grateful to the dead.
Let a soldier's manly form,
Guard the vase his ashes bears,
Truth in living sorrow warm,
Pay a mourning nation's tears;
Fame his praise upon thy wing,
Thro' the world dispersing tell,
In the service of his king,
In his country's cause he fell.

---

### MADRIGAL.  Five Voices.
*T. Linley.*

LET me, careless and unthoughtful lying,
Hear the soft winds above me flying,
   With all the wanton boughs dispute;
   And the more tuneful birds replying,
Till my Delia with her heav'nly song
Silence the wanton boughs, and birds that sing among.

---

### CATCH.  Three Voices.
*Ives.*

COME, honest friends, and jovial boys,
Follow, follow, follow me,
And sing this catch merrily.

## GLEE. Four Voices.

SHAKSPEARE.  Harmonized by JACKSON.

WHERE the bee sucks, there lurk I,
In a cowslip's bell I lie;
There I couch when owls do cry,
On a batt's back do I fly,
After sunset merrily;
Merrily, merrily, shall I live now,
Under the blossom that hangs on the bough.

All we fairies that do run,
By the triple Hecate's beam,
From the presence of the sun;
Follow darkness as a dream.
Over hill, over dale,
Thoro' bush, thoro' briar,
Over park, over pale,
Thoro' flood, thoro' fire.
Merrily, merrily, shall we live now,
Under the blossom that hangs on the bough.

## CATCH. Four Voices.

Purcell.

SOLDIER, soldier take off thy wine,
And shake thy locks as I shake mine;
How can I my poor locks shake,
That have but ten hairs on my pate,
And one of them must go for tythe,
So there remains but four and five;
Four and five, and that makes nine,
Then take off your drink as I take mine.

CATCH.  Three Voices.

*Callcott,* M.B.

HAVE you Sir John Hawkins's History?
Some folks think it quite a mystery?
Music fill'd his wond'rous brain;
How d'ye like him—is it plain?
Both I've read, and must agree,
That Burney's History pleases me.

———

GLEE.  Four Voices.

*Dowland.*

AWAKE, sweet love, thou art return'd,
My heart which long in absence mourn'd,
Lives now in perfect joy.
Only herself hath seemed fair,
She only I could love,
She only drove me to despair,
When she unkind did prove.

———

GLEE.  Three Voices.

*Dr. Cooke.*

ROUND with the glass, boys, as fast as you can,
Since he who dont drink, cannot be a true man;
For if truth is in wine, then 'tis all but a whim,
To think a man true when the wine's not in him:
Drink then and hold it a maxim divine,
There's virtue in truth, and truth in good wine.

### CATCH. Three Voices.

*Hook.*

THE body of great Elizabeth lies here,
To Britain's foes, the scourge, to Britons, dear:
Up to her chin in ruff the waxen figure stands
Grasping the globe, and scepter, with both hands;
Interr'd beneath this place the body lies,
But well earn'd fame and honour never dies.

### CANON. Four Voices.

*Dr. W. Hayes.*

LET'S drink and let's sing together,
In spite of wind and weather,
So let the toast go round;
Come, here's to all honest men,
Fill up your glass,
Drink fair, or drink again.

### ROUND. Three Voices.

*Atterbury.*

SWEET enslaver can you tell,
How I learn'd to love so well;
In the morning when I rise,
If the sunshine strike mine eyes,
All that pleases in his view
Is my hope to look on you.

*GLEE.* Four Voices.

*Atterbury.*

OH thou sweet bird, that sits on some lone spray,
Unseen, amid yon solitary grove,
Fly to my love, and sing thy little lay,
For lays like thine the hardest heart can move;
Sing till all around her soft ey'd pity play,
And one responsive sigh breathe sympathizing love.

*SONG.*

*Dr. Arne.*

BY the gaily circling glass
We can see how minutes pass;
By the hollow cask are told
How the waining night grows old;
Soon, too soon, the busy day,
Drives us from our sports away:
What have we with day to do?
Sons of care 'twas made for you.

*CATCH.* Three Voices.

*Atterbury.*

JOAN said to John, when he stop'd her t'other day,
Pray John let me go, you know I cannot stay;
You always so tieze me and want me to stay;
But tieze me no more, for I must away.
So she left him in spite of all he could say,
Who then could say nought, but pray Joan prithee stay.

### ROUND. Three Voices.
*Purcell.*

UNDER this stone lies Gabriel John,
In the year of our lord one thousand and one;
Cover his head with turf or stone, 'tis all one.
Pray for the soul of gentle John,
If you please you may, or let it alone, 'tis all one.

---

### GLEE. Five Voices.
*Stevens.*

SAD winter pass'd, the leafless grove
Again revives with vernal hue;
Hush'd is the storm that lately strove,
Mild ev'ning sheds her silent dew.
The sun returns with genial ray,
O'er earth the scatter'd seeds are sown;
Fond hope anticipates her day,
And smiles o'er harvests yet unknown.
PHILANTHROPY thy heav'nly ray,
Alike dispelling winter's gloom;
Shall to the virtues life convey,
And rouse them from their early tomb.
Won by the strain thy precepts pour,
Thy pupils emulous shall grow,
Till reason her full light restore,
And joy exult o'er pining woe.

FINIS.

# THE POETRY

OF VARIOUS

# GLEES, SONGS, &c.

AS PERFORMED AT THE

# Harmonists.

LONDON:
PRINTED BY THE PHILANTHROPIC SOCIETY,
ST. GEORGE'S FIELDS.

1813.

# INDEX.

## A.
| | PAGE |
|---|---|
| ALL my sense thy sweetness gained | 58 |
| Adieu, ye jovial youths, who join | 59 |
| Adieu! oh ye bowers! ye shades ever dear | 36 |
| Ah! why suppose deceit is nigh | 26 |
| Awake the lute, the fife, the flute | 34 |

## B.
| | |
|---|---|
| Bronte, Piragmo, e Sterope | 12 |
| Beauties, have you seen a toy | 20 |
| Blest pow'r! here see thy vot'ry bend | 6 |
| By Celia's arbour all the night | 46 |

## C.
| | |
|---|---|
| Crabbed age and youth | 47 |
| Come Clara as the lily fair | 37 |
| Come hither, shepherd's swain | 61 |
| Come buy my cherries, beauteous lasses | 25 |
| Come, let us laugh! let us drink | 14 |
| Cease your music, gentle swains | 41 |
| Child of patient industry | 28 |
| Come bounteous May, in fulness of thy might | 38 |
| Cold is Cadwallo's tongue | 19 |

## D.
| | |
|---|---|
| Doubt thou the stars are fire | 63 |
| Does the harp of Rosa slumber | 32 |
| Die not, fond man, before thy day | 2 |

# INDEX.

## F.

|   | Page |
|---|---|
| Five times, by the taper's light | 21 |
| From the desert's trackless waste | 35 |
| Full well our Christmas sires of old | 27 |
| Fear no danger to ensue | 7 |
| Floreat Æternum | 36 |
| From peace, and social joy, Medusa flies | 5 |

## G.

| Go, lovely rose | 60 |
|---|---|
| Good night, good rest | 39 |
| Genius of Harmony | 42 |
| Gay being born to flutter thro' the day | 35 |
| Give me the sweet delights of love | 6 |

## H.

| Health to my dear, and long unbroken years | 40 |
|---|---|
| Hail, smiling morn! that tips the hills | 26 |
| Hence, away! ye Syrens leave me | 57 |
| Have you seen the virgin snow | 7 |
| Hark! the curfew's solemn sound | 23 |
| Hail, happy meeting | 46 |
| Hail, hallow'd fane | 22 |
| Hail! green fields, and shady woods | 16 |
| Had I but the torrent's might | 13 |
| How calm the ev'ning | 15 |

## I.

| In peace, love tunes the shepherd's read | 31 |
|---|---|
| In tatter'd weed, from town to town | 41 |
| I have been all day looking after | 56 |
| If in that breast, so good, so pure | 55 |
| In the lonely vale of streams | 51 |
| In awful pause | 9 |
| I love to see, at early morn | 43 |
| I know you false, I know you vain | 17 |

# INDEX.

## L.
| | Page |
|---|---|
| L'ape e la serpe spesso | 32 |
| Love in thine eyes for ever plays | 2 |
| Lo! on yon long resounding shore | 30 |
| Laudate nomen Domini | 2 |

## M.
| | |
|---|---|
| Methinks I hear the full celestial choir | 49 |
| Mighty master, hear our sighs | 9 |
| My dear mistress had a heart | 38 |
| Mine be a cot beside a hill | 18 |

## N.
| | |
|---|---|
| Now the hungry lion roars | 64 |

## O.
| | |
|---|---|
| O nightingale that on yon bloomy spray | 30 |
| Oh sov'reign of the willing soul | 42 |
| O snatch me swift | 10 |
| Our bugles sung truce | 29 |
| O happy man | 10 |
| O heav'nly Sympathy | 18 |
| O sanctissima | 63 |
| O Venus! Regina | 52 |
| Over the mountains | 62 |
| Orpheus with his lute | 59 |
| O happy fair | 36 |
| O Nanny, wilt thou gang with me | 12 |

## P.
| | |
|---|---|
| Pray, good Sir | 39 |
| Perfida Clori | 45 |

## Q.
| | |
|---|---|
| Queen of the skies | 50 |
| Queen of the silver bow | 37 |

# INDEX.

## R.
| | PAGE |
|---|---|
| Rise to the battle | 53 |
| Raise the song of mourning | 22 |
| Retire, my love, for it is night | 16 |

## S.
| | |
|---|---|
| Sweet enslaver can you tell | 1 |
| Sweet honey-sucking bees | 1 |
| Stay, Coridon, thou swain | 5 |
| So saith my fair and beautiful Licoris | 5 |
| See what horrid tempests rise | 43 |
| Saints and angels, hear our strains | 54 |
| Sweet muse who lov'st the virgin | 17 |
| Sweet thrush, that makes the vernal year | 8 |
| Soft Cupid, wanton, am'rous boy | 3 |
| Say, mighty love! and teach my song | 21 |
| Sogno, ma te non miro | 24 |
| Spring returns with aspect mild | 48 |

## T.
| | |
|---|---|
| Thy voice, O Harmony | 50 |
| Thou art beautiful | 44 |
| The spring, the pleasant spring | 52 |
| To all that breathe the air | 53 |
| The glories of our birth and state | 54 |
| To what age must we live | 8 |
| Tho' from thy bank of velvet torn | 23 |
| The harp's wild notes | 25 |
| 'Twas you, Sir | 19 |
| To love I wake the silver string | 16 |
| To all you ladies, now at land | 14 |

## V.
| | |
|---|---|
| Virtue, my Emma, is a gem | 55 |
| Vulcan contrive me such a cup | 24 |

# INDEX.

## W.

| | PAGE |
|---|---|
| When Britain on her sea-girt shore | 4 |
| Whence comes my love | 49 |
| With conscious pride I view the band | 20 |
| When lurking love, in ambush lies | 60 |
| What shall we sing; now there are three | 51 |
| When shall we three meet again | 64 |
| With heart and hand come let us join | 48 |
| Would you know my Celia's charms | 51 |
| When to the muses' haunted hill | 11 |
| When at Apollo's hallow'd shrine | 45 |
| Who fed me from her gentle breast | 33 |
| Who is Sylvia? What is she | 40 |
| With sighs, sweet rose | 13 |
| Wherefore burn with vain desires | 15 |
| When Bacchus, Jove's immortal boy | 44 |
| What are sighs? but sorrow's breeze | 47 |
| When time was entwining | 15 |

# POETRY

#### OF VARIOUS

## GLEES, SONGS, &c.

MADRIGAL.—Five Voices.

*Wilbye,* 1609.

Sweet honey-sucking bees, why do ye still
    Surfeit on roses, pinks, and violets?
As if the choicest nectar lay in them,
    Wherewith ye store your curious cabinets.

Ah! make your flight to Melisuavia's lips,
    There may ye revel in ambrosian cheer;
Where smiling roses and sweet lilies sit,
    Keeping their spring-tide graces all the year.

Yet, sweet, take heed, all sweets are hard to get,
Sting not her soft lips, O beware of that!
For if one flaming dart come from her eye,
Was never dart so sharp, ah! then you die.

ROUND.—Three Voices.

*Atterbury.*

Sweet enslaver can you tell
How I learn'd to love so well?
In the morning, when I rise,
If the sunshine strike my eyes,
All that pleases, in his view,
Is my hope to look on you.

## MADRIGAL.—Six Voices.

*Ward,* 1608.

DIE not, fond man, before thy day!
   Love's cold December,
   Will surrender,
To succeeding jocund May:
And then, O then, sorrow shall cease!
   Comforts abounding,
   Cares confounding,
Shall conclude a happy peace.

---

## DUETTO.

COWLEY.                *Jackson.*

LOVE in thine eyes for ever plays,
He in thy snowy bosom strays,
He makes thy rosy lips his care;
And walks the mazes of thy hair;
Love dwells in ev'ry outward part,
But, ah! he never touch'd thy heart!
How diff'rent is my fate from thine,
No outward marks of love are mine;
My brow is clouded by despair,
And grief, Love's bitter foe, is there;
But deep within my glowing soul,
He reigns and rules without controul.

---

## MOTETT.—Four Voices.

*Dr. Tye,* 1553.

LAUDATE nomen Domini, vos Servi Domini,
Ab ortu solis usque ad occasum ejus.
Decreta Dei justa sunt, et cor exhilarant.
Laudate Deum, Principes, et omnes populi.

## GLEE.—Three Voices.

PRIOR.              *Travers.*

Soft Cupid, wanton, am'rous boy,
    The other day, mov'd with my lyre;
In flatt'ring accents spoke his joy,
    And utter'd thus his fond desire:
O raise thy voice! one song I ask;
    Touch then th' harmonious string;
To Thyrsis easy is the task,
    Who can so sweetly play and sing.

Two kisses from my mother dear,
    Thyrsis, thy due reward shall be;
None like beauty's queen is fair,
    Paris has vouch'd this truth for me.
I strait reply'd, thou know'st alone
    That brightest Chloe rules my breast;
I'll sing thee two instead of one,
    If thou'lt be kind, and make me blest.

One kiss from Chloe's lips, no more
    I crave; he promis'd me success;
I play'd with all my skill and pow'r,
    My glowing passion to express.
But, O my Chloe, beauteous maid!
    Wilt thou the wish'd reward bestow?
Wilt thou make good what Love has said,
    And by thy grant his power show?
            *Da Capo.* I play'd, &c.

## THE WOODEN WALLS OF ENGLAND.
### GLEE.—Three Voices and Chorus.
*Dr. Arne.*

When Britain, on her sea-girt shore,
    Her ancient druids erst address'd;
What aid, she cry'd, shall I implore,
    What best defence by numbers press'd?
Tho' hostile nations round thee rise,
    The mystic oracles reply'd,
And view thine isle with envious eyes;
    Their threats defy, their rage deride:
Nor fear invasion from those adverse Gauls,
Britain's best bulwarks are her Wooden Walls.

Thine oaks, descending to the main,
    With floating forts shall stem the tide;
Asserting Britain's liquid reign,
    Where'er her thund'ring navy rides.
Nor less to peaceful arts inclin'd,
    Where commerce opens all her stores;
In social bands shall league mankind,
    And join the sea divided shores:
Spread then thy sails where naval glory calls,
Britain's best bulwarks are her Wooden Walls.

Hail, happy isle! what tho' thy vales
    No wine impurpled tribute yield;
Nor fann'd with odour breathing gales,
    Nor crops spontaneous glad the field:
Yet liberty, rewards the toil
    Of industry, to labour prone;
Who jocund ploughs the grateful soil,
    And reaps the harvest she has sown:
While other realms tyrannic sway enthrals,
Britain's best bulwarks are her Wooden Walls.

## MADRIGAL.—Six Voices.

*Lucca Marenzio, 1580.*

So saith my fair and beautiful Licoris,
When now and then she talketh
With me of love:
Love is a sprite that walketh,
That soars and flies,
And none alive can hold him,
Nor touch him, nor behold him;
Yet, when her eyes she turneth,
I spy where he sojourneth;
In her eyes, there he flies,
But none can catch him,
Till from her lips he fetch him.

## MADRIGAL.—Six Voices.

*Wilbye, 1609.*

Stay, Coridon, thou swain,
  Talk not so soon of dying;
What tho' thy heart be slain,
  What tho' thy love be flying!
She threatens thee, but dares not strike,
Thy nymph is light, and shadow-like,
For if thou follow her, she'll fly from thee,
But if thou fly from her, she'll follow thee.

## GLEE.—Four Voices.

*S. Webbe, Jun.*

From peace, and social joy, Medusa flies;
And loves to hear the storm of anger rise:
Thus hags and witches hate the smiles of day,
Sport in loud thunder, and in tempest play.

## CATCH.—Three Voices.

*Dr. Harrington.*

Give me the sweet delights of love,
Let not anxious care destroy them;
O! how divine, still to enjoy them!
Pure are the blessings love bestowing,
Peace and harmony ever flowing:
A smoky house, a failing trade,
Six squalling brats, and a scolding jade.

## INVOCATION TO LOVE.
## GLEE.—Four Voices.

*S. Paxton.   Medal, 1784.*

Blest pow'r! here see thy vot'ry bend
   Despondent at thy shrine;
O may my Celia's breast ne'er feel
   The pain that tortures mine.

Tell her the flame that artless burns,
   All pure within my breast;
On her relies each hope and fear,
   Which she alone can rest.

O bid her own why thus her heart
   Relentless hears my pain;
And kindly wing thy golden dart,
   To make her love again.

## RONDEAU.—Four Voices.

*Purcel, 1677.*

Fear no danger to ensue,
The hero loves as well as you.
Ever gentle, ever smiling,
And the cares of life beguiling:
Fear no danger to ensue,
The hero loves as well as you.
Cupids strew your paths with flow'rs,
Gather'd from Elysian bow'rs:
Fear no danger to ensue,
The hero loves as well as you.

---

## TUDOR AND MALVINA.
### GLEE.—Four Voices.

*Dr. Cooke.*

Have you seen the virgin snow,
That tops old Aran's peering brow?
Or lucid webby insect spun
Purpureal gleam in summer sun?
With such, yet far diviner light,
Malvina hits the dazzled sight:
The Guerdon such, can Tudor's breast
Dare to court ignoble rest?
Have you e'er on barren strand,
Ta'en your solitary stand?
And seen the whirlwind's spirit sped
O'er the dark green billowy bed?
Glowing in the thickest fight,
Such resistless Tudor's might.

## GLEE.—Four Voices.

*Danby.*

Sweet thrush, that makes the vernal year
Sweeter than Flora can appear,
As Philomel attends thy lay,
She envies the return of day.
The tuneful lyre, and swelling flute,
At thy rich warbling shall be mute.
Vocal minstrel, thy soft lay
Treasures up and ends the May.
Hark! how the blackbird wooes his love,
The skill'd musician of the grove;
On thorn, as perch'd, he nobly sings
A cadence for the best of kings;
Sublime and gay, soft and serene,
A virginal to hail a queen.
Nature's music thus improves
All the graces and the loves.

## GLEE.—Four Voices.

Cumberland. *Stevens.*

*(With a Double Accompaniment.)*

To what age must we live without love?
    If we out stay the time
    Of our youth's happy prime,
'Tis an age that will never improve.

When the sweet early rose is in bloom,
    If the minutes pass by
    Till it wither and die,
Poor Rose! where is then its perfume.
              *Da Capo.*

## DIALOGUE AND CHORUS.—Four Voices.
*Dibdin.*

*(Arranged by Stevens.)*

EVIL SPIRITS.

MIGHTY master, hear our sighs,
  Let thy slaves be free!
With folded hands, and lifted eyes,
  We call to thee.
Oh! end the strife; Oh! grant us life;
Grant us still more, sweet liberty!

BONORO *(A Magician.)*

Wretched, base, and blind
Evil spirits, peace! your clamours cease!
By guilt confin'd, in vain your mind
Pants for freedom's happy hour.
In pity to your pains,
I loos'd your chains,
But circumscrib'd your pow'r,
In pity to mankind.

---

## GLEE.—Five Voices.
HOMER                 *Dr. Callcott.*

IN awful pause, while Heav'n's revenge is slow,
Jove but prepares to strike a fiercer blow.
That day shall come, that great avenging day,
When Troy's proud glories in the dust shall lay;
When Priam's pow'rs, and Priam's self shall fall,
And one prodigious ruin swallow all.
I see the God, already, from the pole,
Bare his red arm, and bid the thunder roll;
I see th' eternal all his fury shed,
And shake his ægis o'er the guilty head.

## GLEE.—Six Voices.

Tasso.                                         *J. S. Smith.*

### Syrens.

O happy man! when youth reigns o'er thy hours,
And strews the paths of life with smiling flow'rs;
Learn the sweet fruit each season yields to prize,
Who follows nature, he alone is wise.

### Anti-Syrens.

Think not true pleasure plac'd in flow'ry fields,
In transient joys, which fading beauty yields;
Far, far, from hence, thy gen'rous soul must rise,
And gain, by virtuous deeds, th' immortal prize!

### Syrens.

Who follows pleasure, he alone is wise.

### Anti-Syrens.

Who follows virtue, he is great and wise.

---

## GLEE.—Five Voices.

*Dr. Callcott.*

O snatch me swift from these tempestuous scenes,
To where life knows not what distraction means:
To where religion, peace, and comfort dwell,
And cheer with heartfelt rays my lonely cell.
Yet if it please thee best, thou pow'r supreme,
My bark to drive thro' life's more rapid stream;
If low'ring storms my destin'd course attend,
And ocean rages till my days shall end.
Let ocean rage, let storms indignant roar,
I bow submissive, and resign'd adore.

GLEE.—Five Voices.

J. S. Smith.

When to the muses' haunted hill,
Their laurel groves, and that pure rill
Which poets drink of old, drew nigh
The goddess of the azure eye.
To welcome her, th' immortal choir,
Uprais'd the voice, and struck the lyre;
The pow'rs of heav'nly sound were all display'd,
To greet with honour due, the sire born maid.
First in responsive fugue was shewn,
    The energy of artful song;
Then closing full, in richer tone,
    Slow modulation march'd along:
'Twas then in union, three times three,
They sung their first celestial glee;
    Sometimes with luxuriant airs,
    Or singing singly, or in pairs,
They wanton'd in the wilds of sound:
    And last, with symphony complete,
    Tho' full and strong, divinely sweet,
They made their notes from Pindus' rocks rebound.
Shall wisdom only claim the lay?
    To beauty too, the song is due,
And ev'ry tribute harmony can pay.
Inspir'd by that celestial throng;
The festive strain we'll lead along;
To welcome beauty to the seats of song.

## GLEE.—Four Voices.

Dr. Percy. *Carter & Harrison.*

O Nanny, wilt thou gang with me,
   Nor sigh to leave the flaunting town?
Can silent glens have charms for thee,
   The lowly cot, and russet gown?
No longer drest in silken sheen,
   No longer deck'd with jewels rare,
Say, canst thou quit the busy scene,
   Where thou art fairest of the fair?

And when at last thy love shall die,
   Wilt thou receive his parting breath?
Wilt thou repress each struggling sigh,
   And cheer with smiles the bed of death?
And wilt thou o'er his breathless clay
   Strew flow'rs, and drop the tender tear?
Nor then regret those scenes so gay,
   Where thou wert fairest of the fair.

## GLEE.—Three Voices.

*Spofforth.*

Bronte, Piragmo, e Sterope,
Del cor m'han fatto incudine,
E del gran Giove il folgore
Battendo in esso van.

Eolo vi mena il mantice,
Plutone il fuoco stuzzica,
Le Furie il fulmin temprano,
I Fati a Giove il dan.

### GLEE.—Four Voices.
*Dr. Callcott.*

With sighs, sweet rose! I mark thy faded form,
　So late bedeck'd with many a flow'ret gay;
Thy tender frame has shrunk beneath the storm,
　And all thy charms are verging to decay:
Yet, whilst I mourn, lov'd plant, thy early doom,
　Poor hapless victim of the pitying shower!
Reflection whispers, thou again shalt bloom,
　And joyful feel the sun's reviving power.
Returning spring thy beauties shall renew,
　Again the breeze shall waft thy sweets along;
Thy fragrant flow'rs, enchanting to the view,
　Shall rise for ever in the poet's song:
Whilst I, with unavailing tears deplore
Dear happy hours, that can return no more.

### GLEE.—Four Voices.
*R. Cooke.*

Had I but the torrent's might,
With headlong rage and wild affright,
On Deira's squadrons hurl'd,
To rush and sweep them from the world.
To Mona's vales, in glittering row,
Twice ten hundred warriors go;
Flush'd with mirth and hope they burn,
But none from Mona's vales return;
Save I, the meanest of them all,
Who live to sing and weep their **fall**.

### ROUND.—Three Voices.
*Dr. Green.*

Come, let us laugh! let us drink, let us sing!
The winter to us is as good as the spring;
We care not a feather for wind or for weather,
By night and day we sport and play,
Conferring our notes together.

---

### GLEE.—Three Voices.
Earl of Dorset.             *Dr. Callcott.*

To all you ladies, now at land,
   We men at sea indite;
But first would have you understand,
   How hard it is to write:
The muses now, and Neptune too,
We must implore to write to you.
                With a fal lal lal lal la.

In justice you cannot refuse,
   To think of our distress;
When we for hopes of honour lose,
   Our certain happiness:
All these designs are but to prove,
Ourselves more worthy of your love.
                With a fal lal lal lal la.

And now we've told you all our loves,
   And likewise all our fears;
In hopes this declaration moves,
   Some pity for our tears:
Let's hear of no inconstancy,
We have enough of that at sea.
                With a fal lal lal lal la.

### GLEE.—Three Voices.

*Dr. Callcott.*

WHEN Time was entwining the garland of years,
   Which to crown my beloved was giv'n;
Tho' some of the leaves might be sullied with tears,
   Yet the flow'rs were all gather'd in heav'n:
And long may this garland be sweet to the eye,
   May its verdure for ever be new;
Young Love shall enrich it with many a sigh,
   And Pity shall nurse it with dew.

### GLEE.—Four Voices.

*Spofforth.*

How calm the ev'ning! see the falling day,
Gilds ev'ry mountain with a ruddy ray;
In gentle sighs the softly whisp'ring breeze,
Salutes the flow'rs, and waves the trembling trees.

### GLEE.—Five Voices.

HORACE.                  *Stevens.*

WHEREFORE burn with vain desires?
Few the things that life requires;
Youth with rapid swiftness flies,
Beauty's blossom quickly dies.

Thus, beneath this lofty shade,
Thus, in careless freedom laid;
While we are with roses crown'd,
Let the cheerful bowl go round.

### ROUND.—Three Voices.
*Dr. Green.*

Hail! green fields, and shady woods,
Hail! chrystal streams, that still run pure;
Hail! Nature's uncorrupted goods,
Where virtue only dwells secure;
Free from vice, and free from care,
Age has no pain nor youth a snare.

---

### GLEE.—Four Voices.
Ossian.              *Horsley, M.B.*

Retire, my love, for it is night, and the dark winds sigh in thy hair. Retire, my love, to the hall of my feasts. Cease a little while, O wind! Stream be thou silent a while. Let my steps be heard on the heath. My love is fairer than the light; more pleasant than the gale of the hill, which sighs on the hunter's ear.

---

### MADRIGAL.—Eight Voices.
Anacreon.              *Webbe.*

To love I wake the silver string,
And of his soft dominion sing;
A wreath of flow'rs adorn his brow
The sweetest, fairest, flow'rs that blow:
All mortals own his mighty sway,
And him the gods above obey.

### GLEE.—Five Voices.

Mrs. OPIE.                  Horsley, M. B.

I know you false, I know you vain,
Yet still I cannot break my chain :
Though with those lips so sweetly smiling,
Those eyes so bright and so beguiling;
On every youth by turns you smile,
And every youth by turns beguile;
Yet still enchant and still deceive me,
Do all things, fatal fair, but leave me.

Still let me in those sparkling eyes,
Trace all your feelings as they rise :
Still from those lips in crimson swelling,
Which seem of soft delight the dwelling;
Catch tones of sweetness, which the soul,
In fetters ever new, controul;
Nor let my starts of passion grieve thee,
Tho' death to stay, 'twere death to leave thee.

---

### GLEE.—Five Voices.

                                   *Stevens.*

Sweet muse who lov'st the virgin spring,
Hither thy sunny flow'rets bring;
And let thy richest chaplet shed
Its fragrance round my Handel's head.

Now string the tuneful lyre again,
Let all thy sisters raise the strain;
And consecrate to deathless fame,
My lov'd, my honour'd, Handel's name.

C

## GLEE.—Four Voices.

Rogers. *Horsley, M. B.*

Mine be a cot beside a hill,
   A bee hive's hum shall sooth my ear;
A willing brook that turns a mill,
   With many a fall shall linger near;
The swallow oft beneath my thatch,
   Shall twitter from her clay built nest;
Oft shall the pilgrim lift the latch,
   And share my meal a welcome guest:

Around my ivied porch shall spring,
   Each fragrant flow'r that drinks the dew;
And Lucy at her wheel shall sing
   In russet gown and apron blue.
The village church, among the trees,
   Where first our marriage vows were giv'n;
With merry peal shall swell the breeze;
   And point with taper spire to heav'n.

---

## GLEE.—Four Voices.

Birch. *Attwood.*

O heav'nly Sympathy, of aspect mild!
Sister of Pity! Nature's fav'rite child!
Queen of the ling'ring tear, that loves to lie
On beauty's cheek, or dims the warrior's eye;
With soothing sighs and radiance all serene,
Soften our fate and brighten all the scene;
To Love's own cause thy magic influence lend,
On healing wings, celestial maid, descend!

## GLEE.—Five Voices.

GRAY.   Horsley, M. B.

Cold is Cadwallo's tongue,
  That hush'd the stormy main;
Brave Urien sleeps upon his craggy bed:
  Mountains, ye mourn in vain.
Dear lost companions of my tuneful art,
  Dear, as the light that visits these sad eyes,
Dear as the ruddy drops that warm my heart,
  Ye died amidst your dying country's cries;
No more I weep. They do but sleep.
  On yonder cliff, a grisly band
I see them sit, they linger yet,
  Avengers of their native land:
With me in dreadful harmony they join,
And weave, with bloody hands, the tissue of thy line.

---

## CATCH.—Three Voices.

'Twas you, Sir!
I tell you nothing new, Sir,
'Twas you that kiss'd the pretty girl;
'Twas you, Sir, you.
'Tis true, Sir;
You look so very blue, Sir,
I'm sure you kiss'd the pretty girl;
'Tis true, Sir, true.
Oh, Sir! no, Sir!
How can you wrong me so, Sir?
I did not kiss the pretty girl;
But I know who.

## GLEE.—Five Voices.

BEN JONSON.      *Evans. Glee Club Prize,* 1811.

BEAUTIES, have you seen a toy,
Called love, a little boy,
Almost naked, wanton, blind;
Cruel now; and then as kind?
If he be amongst you, say;
He is Venus' run away.

She, that will but now discover
Where this winged wag doth hover,
Shall this night receive a kiss,
How and where herself could wish:
But who brings him to his mother
Shall have that kiss, and another.
                               *Da Capo.*

---

## GLEE.—Four Voices.

                                        *Stevens.*

WITH conscious pride I view the band
Of faithful friends that round me stand;
With pride exult that I alone,
Can join these scatter'd gems in one;
Rejoic'd to be the silken line
On which these pearls united shine.

'Tis mine their inmost souls to see,
Unlock'd is ev'ry heart to me;
To me they cling, on me they rest,
I hold a place in ev'ry breast:
Rejoic'd to be the silken line
On which these pearls united shine.

## GLEE.—Four Voices.

Dr. Watts.             Evans.

Say, mighty love! and teach my song,
To whom thy sweetest joys belong,
    And who the happy pairs;
Whose yielding hearts, and joining hands,
Find blessings twisted with their bands,
    To soften all their cares?

Not the mad tribe that hell inspires,
With wanton flames, those raging fires,
    The purer bliss destroy:
On Etna's top let furies wed,
And sheets of lightning deck their bed,
    T'improve the burning joy.

Two kindred souls, alone must meet,
'Tis friendship makes the bondage sweet,
    And feeds their mutual loves;
Bright Venus on her rolling throne,
Is drawn by gentlest birds alone,
    And Cupids' yoke the doves.

---

## GLEE.—Four Voices.

            Storace.

Five times, by the taper's light,
The hourglass I have turn'd to-night.
Where's father?—he's gone out to roam;
    If he have luck,
    He'll bring a buck
Upon his lusty shoulders home.
Hark! from the woodland vale below
The distant bell sounds dull and slow.

## LINES ON WESTMINSTER ABBEY.
### GLEE.—Four Voices.
*Lord Mornington.*

Hail, hallow'd fane! amid'st whose mould'ring shrines,
　Her vigils musing melancholy keeps;
Upon her arm her harrow'd cheek reclines,
　And o'er the spoils of human grandeur weeps!

Hail, awful edifice! thine ailes along,
　In contemplation wrapt, O let me stray;
And stealing from the idle busy throng,
　Serenely meditate the moral lay.

What pleasing sadness fills my thoughtful breast,
　When e'er my steps these vaulted mansions trace;
Where, in their silent tombs, for ever rest,
　The honour'd ashes of the British race.

---

### GLEE.—Five Voices and Chorus.
*Ossian.*　　　　　　　　　　　　　　　*Stevens.*

Raise the song of mourning, O Bards! over the land of strangers! they have but fall'n before us;—for one day we must fall. When thou, sun of heav'n! shalt fail;—if thou shalt fail, thou mighty light! If thy brightness is for a season, our fame shall survive thy beams.—Raise the song of mourning over the land of strangers! they have but fall'n before us; —for one day we must fall.

　Raise the song! Send round the shell! Let joy be heard in the hall! Let the night pass away in song, and the morning return with joy! Let the blast of the desert come;—We shall be renown'd in our day! the mark of our arm shall be in battle;—our name in the song of bards.

## TO A VIOLET.
### GLEE.—Five Voices.
*Stevens.*

Tho' from thy bank of velvet torn,
   Hang not, fair flow'r, thy drooping crest;
On Anna's bosom thou shalt find
   A softer, sweeter, bed of rest.

Tho' from mild zephyr's kiss no more,
   Ambrosial balms thou shalt inhale,
Her gentle breath, whene'er she sighs,
   Shall fan thee with a purer gale.
                Tho' from thy bank, &c.

But thou be grateful for that bliss,
   For which in vain a thousand burn,
And as thou stealest sweets from her,
   Give back thy choicest in return.
                *Da Capo.*

---

### GLEE.—Four Voices.
*Attwood.*

Hark! the curfew's solemn sound!
Silent darkness spreads around;
Heavy it beats on the lover's heart,
   Who leaves with a sigh his tale half told:
The poring monk and his books must part,
   And fearful the miser locks his gold.
Now while labour sleeps, and charmed sorrow,
     O'er the dewy green,
        By the glow-worm's light,
        Dance the elves of night,
     Unheard, unseen:
Yet where their midnight pranks have been,
The circled turf will betray to-morrow.

## GLEE.—Four Voices.
*Evans.*

VULCAN contrive me such a cup,
    As Nestor us'd of old?
Try all your skill to trim it up,
    And deck it round with gold:
Make it so large that fill'd with sack,
    Up to the sparkling brim,
Vast toasts on the delicious lake,
    Like ships at sea may swim?
Carve me thereon a spreading vine,
    Then add two lovely boys;
Their limbs in am'rous folds entwine,
    The type of future joys.
Cupid and Bacchus my gods are,
    May drink and love still reign;
With wine I'll wash away my care
    And then to love again.

---

## GLEE.—Three Voices.
*Trajetta.*

SOGNO, ma te non miro
Sempre nè sogni miei;
Mi desto, e tu non sei
Il primo mio pensier.

Lungi date m'aggiro,
Senza bramarti mai,
Son teco, e non mi fai
Nè pena nè piacer.

## DUBLIN CRIES.
### CATCH.—Four Voices.
*Sir John Stevenson.*

Come buy my cherries, beauteous lasses,
Fresh from the garden pluck'd by me;
All on a summer's day so gay
You hear the Dublin cries:
Knives ground here by me;
Fine apples and choice pears,
Eat boys, forget your cares,
Sweep! sweep! sweep! sweep!
Fruit in abundance sold by me,
Fruit in abundance here you see,
Fine parsnips, fine carrots, and choice beans;
Whey, fine sweet whey, come taste my whey,
Fine radish, fine lettuce, sold by me.

---

### GLEE.—Four Voices.
Scott.                                            *Attwood.*
*(With a Double Accompaniment.)*

The harp's wild notes, tho' hush'd the song,
The mimic march of death prolong,
Now seems it far, and now a near,
Now meets, and now eludes the ear;
Now seems some mountain's side to sweep,
Now faintly dies in vallies deep;
Now seems as if some minstrel's wail,
Now the sad requiem loads the gale;
Last o'er the warrior's closing grave,
Rung the full choir in choral stave.

## GLEE.—Four Voices.

*Spofforth*

Hail, smiling morn! that tips the hills with gold,
Whose rosy fingers ope the gates of day!
Who the gay face of Nature doth unfold,
At whose bright presence darkness flies away.

        Hail! Hail!

---

## GLEE.—Three Voices.

*Attwood.*

Ah! why suppose deceit is nigh,
 While Carlos is in view?
Ah! why suppose he heaves a sigh
 For any fair but you?

Those charms alone my heart enslave;
 For those my wishes pine:
I'd give up all this side the grave,
 Could I but call thee mine.

Ah! why with looks of love persuade,
 Which too successful woo?
Ah! why thus tempt a simple maid,
 Too well inclin'd to you?

Let honour consecrate the band
 Of love 'twixt you and me;
And, till a parent gives this hand,
 My heart I'll keep for thee.

## CHRISTMAS EVE.
### GLEE.—Three Voices.

Scott.                    *Attwood.*

Full well our Christmas sires of old,
Lov'd, when the year its course had roll'd,
And brought blithe Christmas back again;
With all its hospitable train.
Domestic and religious rite
Gave honour to the holy night.
On Christmas-eve the bells were rung;
On Christmas-eve the mass was sung:
That only night, in all the year,
Saw the stol'd priest the chalice rear.
The damsel donn'd her kirtle sheen;
The hall was dress'd with holly green;
Forth to the wood did merry men go,
To gather in the misletoe:
Then open'd wide the Baron's hall,
To vassal, tenant, serf, and all;
Power laid his rod of rule aside,
And ceremony doff'd his pride.
The heir, with roses in his shoes,
That night might village part'ner chuse;
The lord, underogating, share
The vulgar game of "Post and Pair."
All hail'd, with uncontrol'd delight,
And general voice, the happy night,
That to the cottage, and the crown,
Brought tidings of salvation down.

## GLEE.

Charlotte Smith.                                      *Attwood.*

Child of patient industry,
Little, active, busy bee,
Thou art out at early morn,
Just as the op'ning flow'rs are born;
Among the green and grass meads,
Where the cowslips hang their heads,
Or by hedge-rows, while the dew
Glitters on the hare-bell blue:
But when the meadows shall be mown,
And summer's garlands overblown;
Then come, thou little busy bee,
And let thy homestead be with me;
There, shelter'd in thy straw-built hive,
In my garden thou shalt thrive;
And that garden shall supply
Thy delicious alchymy;
Then for thee in autumn blows
The India pink, and latest rose;
The mignionette perfumes the air,
And stocks, unfading flowers, are there.
Yet fear not, when the tempests come,
And drive thee to thy waxen home,
That I shall then most treach'rously,
For thy honey murder thee.
Ah, no! throughout the winter drear
I'll feed thee, that another year
Thou may'st renew thy industry
Among the flowers, thou busy bee.

## THE SOLDIER'S DREAM.
### SONG.

*Attwood.*

Our bugles sung truce, for the night cloud had lower'd,
    And the centinel stars set their watch in the sky;
And thousands had sunk on the ground overpower'd,
    The weary to sleep, and the wounded to die.

When, reposing that night on my pallet of straw,
    By the wolf scaring faggot that guarded the slain,
At the dead of the night a sweet vision I saw,
    And twice ere the cock crew I dream't it again.

Methought from the battle-field's dreadful array,
    Far, far, I had roam'd on a desolate track,
Till autumn and sunshine arose on the way,
    To the home of my fathers that welcom'd me back.

I flew to the pleasant fields travers'd so oft,
    In life's morning march, when my bosom was young;
I heard my own mountain goats bleating aloft,
    And knew the sweet strain that the corn reaper's sung.

Then pledg'd we the wine cup, and fondly I swore,
    From my home and my weeping friends never to part;
My little ones kiss'd me a thousand times o'er,
    And my wife sobb'd aloud, in the fulness of heart.

Stay, stay with us, rest; thou art weary and worn:
    And fain was the war-broken soldier to stay;
But sorrow return'd with the dawning of morn,
    And the voice in my dreaming ear melted away.

## GLEE.—Five Voices.

MILTON.  *Stevens.*

O NIGHTINGALE that on yon bloomy spray,
Warblest at eve when all the woods are still :
Thou with fresh hope the lover's heart dost fill,
While the jolly hours lead on propitious May.

---

## GLEE.—Five Voices.

*Horsley, M. B.*

LO ! on yon long resounding shore,
   Where the rock totters o'er the headlong deep ;
What phantoms bath'd in infant gore
   Stand mutt'ring o'er the dizzy steep !
Their murmur shakes the zephyr's wing,
   The storm obeys their pow'rful spell :
   See from his gloomy cell
Fierce winter starts :
   His scowling eye
Blots the fair mantle of the breathing spring,
   And tow'rs along the ruffled sky.
To the deep vault the yelling harpies run,
   Its yawning mouth receives th' infernal crew ;
Dim, thro' the black gloom, winks the glimm'ring sun,
   And the pale furnace gleams with brimstone blue.
Hell howls, and fiends, that join the dire acclaim,
Dance on the bubbling tide and point the livid flame.

## GLEE.—Four Voices.

DIMOND. *Attwood.*

YE visions wild, Hope's fairy train!
    That o'er my bosom rove;
Your soft dominion still retain,
    And murmur tales of love.

Still hush to rest the heaving sigh,
    Still fondly wipe the tear,
With dear delusion soothe the eye,
    And chase the frowns of fear.

With balmy touch revive the bloom
    Of Fancy's wither'd wreath,
Bid each frail flow'r its tint resume,
    And fresher incense breathe.

Blest hope! ah whence this fluttering, say!
    By thee I feel restor'd;
My bosom owns thy genial sway,
    And heaves to greet its lord.

---

## GLEE.—Three Voices.

SCOTT. *Attwood.*

*(With a Double Accompaniment.)*

IN peace, Love tunes the shepherd's reed;
In war, he mounts the warrior's steed;
In halls, in gay attire is seen;
In hamlets, dances on the green;
Love rules the court, the camp, the grove,
All men below, and saints above;
For love is heav'n, and heav'n is love!

## GLEE.—Four Voices.

*Attwood.*

Does the harp of Rosa slumber?
Once it breath'd the sweetest number:
Never does a wilder song
Steal the breezy lyre along;
When the wind in odours dying,
Woos it with enamour'd sighing.

Does the harp of Rosa cease?
Once it told the tale of peace,
To her lover's throbbing breast,
Then she was divinely blest.
Ah! but Rosa loves no more,
Therefore Rosa's song is o'er,
And her harp neglected lies,
And her boy forgotten sighs;
Silent harp, forgotten lover,
Rosa's love and song are over.

---

## GLEE.—Four Voices.

*Spofforth.*

L'ape e la serpe spesso
Suggon l'istesso umore;
Ma l'alimento istesso
Cangiando in lor si va.

Che della serpe in seno
Il fior si fa veleno:
In sen dell'ape il fiore
Dolce liquor si fa.

## GLEE.—Four Voices.

*Attwood.*

Who fed me from her gentle breast,
And hush'd me in her arms to rest,
And on my cheeks sweet kisses prest?
          My Mother.

When sleep forsook my open eye,
Who was it sung sweet lullaby,
And rock'd me that I should not cry?
          My Mother.

Who sat and watch'd my infant head,
When sleeping on my cradle bed,
And tears of sweet affection shed?
          My Mother.

When pain and sickness made me cry,
Who gaz'd upon my heavy eye,
And wept for fear that I should die?
          My Mother.

And can I ever cease to be,
Affectionate and kind to thee,
Who was so very kind to me:
          My Mother.

When thou art feeble, old, and grey,
My healthy arm shall be thy stay;
And I will soothe thy pains away:
          My Mother.

## THE FIRST OF MAY.
### GLEE.—Three Voices.
*(With a Double Accompaniment.)*

*Attwood.*

AWAKE the lute,
The fife, the flute,
The doric reed, the choral song :
　Come nymphs and swains,
　To pleasures strains,
Lead the fantastic dance along;
　For lo ! to-day
　The blue ey'd May,
Once more her jocund reign renews;
　And love and mirth,
　O'er laughing earth,
Their blended influence wide diffuse.
　The turtle coos,
　The blackbird woos,
His sooty mate in grove and glen;
　The snipe aloft,
　With warbling soft,
His list'ning partner of the fen.
　The chrystal stream,
　Invites the beam,
Upon its bosom to recline;
　The beam descends,
　New lustre lends,
The silver streams meand'ring line :
　The blooming race,
　Expands apace,

Till hill and dale with beauty glow;
    Light o'er the sky,
    The thin clouds fly,
While soft the genial breezes blow.
    Now cull a wreath,
    That balm shall breathe,
Fresh from the dew'y couch of morn;
    Meet homage pay,
    To lovely May,
And all her sylvan shrine adorn.
              Awake the lute, &c.

## ARAB GLEE.—Six Voices.

*Attwood.*

From the desert's trackless waste,
Silent and swift we Arabs stray;
Hopes of plunder urge our haste,
Hopes of conquest point the way.

## *THE BUTTERFLY.*
## DUETTO.

*J. B. Sale.*

Gay being born to flutter thro' the day,
    Sport in the sunshine of the present hour;
On the sweet rose, thy painted wings display,
    And cull the fragrance of the op'ning flow'r.
Time hastens on, the summer ends too soon,
    Take then the rosy minutes as they fly;
For soon, alas! your little life is gone,
    To-day you sparkle, and to-morrow die.

## GLEE.—Three Voices.
*Allwood.*

Adieu! oh ye bowers! ye shades ever dear!
  Adieu! ye lov'd haunts, once so gay!
For ever farewell to the smiles of the year!
  Farewell to the smiles of the may!
Adieu! oh ye songsters that people yon grove!
  With sorrow I bid you depart;
Adieu to the joy of contentment and love!
  Oh well-a-day! sighs my poor heart.
No more may I traverse, as fancy shall lead,
  The valley, or follow the stream:
No more, as I wander along the gay mead,
  Must Damon and love be my theme.
The dream of delusion which hope would invite,
  No longer must rapture impart;
For lost is the youth, who alone could delight:
  Oh well-a-day! sighs my poor heart.

## GLEE.—Three Voices.
SHAKESPEARE. *Shield.*

O happy fair!
Your eyes are lode-stars; and your tongue's sweet air
More tuneable than lark to shepherd's ear,
When wheat is green, when hawthorn buds appear.

## AN ANCIENT CHARTERHOUSE SENTIMENT.
Four Voices and Chorus.
*Stevens.*

Floreat Æternùm Carthusiana domus.
                    Amen.

### GLEE.—Four Voices.
*Spofforth.*

Come Clara as the lily fair,
  Blushing like the dew-kiss'd rose;
Yon murm'ring rill shall soothe your ear,
  And Strephon sigh thee to repose.

What tho' by persecuting fate,
  The charms of luxury's denied;
The empty farce of servile state,
  And all the purple train of pride:

Yet if with me you seek the plain,
  With me enjoy the rural cot;
A happy, tho' a humble swain,
  Ye proud and great, I scorn your lot.

### GLEE.—Four Voices.
*Hindle, M. B.*

Queen of the silver bow! by thy pale beam
  Alone and pensive I delight to stray;
And watch thy shadow trembling in the stream,
  Or mark the floating clouds that cross thy way.
Still while I gaze, thy mild and placid light
  Sheds a soft calm upon my troubled breast;
And oft I think, fair planet of the night,
  That in thy orb the wretched may have rest.
The suff'rers of the earth, perhaps, may go,
  Releas'd by death, to thy benignant sphere;
And the sad children of despair and woe,
  Forget in thee their cup of sorrow here:
Oh that I soon may reach thy world serene!
Poor wearied pilgrim in this toiling scene!

GLEE.—Four Voices.

*Spofforth.*

My dear mistress had a heart
  Soft as those kind looks she gave me;
When with love's resistless art,
  And her eyes she did enslave me:
But her constancy's so weak,
  She's so wild and apt to wander;
That my jealous heart would break,
  Should we live one day asunder.

Melting joys about her move,
  Killing pleasures, wounding blisses!
She can dress her eyes in love,
  And her lips can arm with kisses:
Angels listen when she speaks!
  She's my delight, all mankind's wonder!
But my jealous heart would break,
  Should we live one day asunder.

---

GLEE.—Four Voices.

*Spofforth.*

Come, bounteous May, in fulness of thy might,
  Lead briskly on, the mirth-infusing hours;
All recent from the bosom of delight,
  With nectar nurtur'd, and involv'd in flow'rs.
By Spring's sweet blush, by Nature's teeming womb,
By Hebe's dimply smile, by Flora's bloom,
By Venus' self, for Venus self demands thee, come?

## GLEE.—Five Voices.

**Shakespeare.** *Spofforth.*

Good night, good rest; ah! neither be my share:
  She bade good night, that kept my rest away;
And daft me to a cabin hang'd with care,
  To descant on the doubts of my decay.
Farewell! (quoth she) and come again to-morrow;
Farewell! I could not, for I supp'd with sorrow.

Yet, at my parting, sweetly did she smile,
  In scorn, or friendship, nill I conster whether:
It may be she joy'd to jest at my exile;
  It may be again to make me wander thither.
Sorrow chang'd to solace, and solace mixt with sorrow;
For why? she sigh'd, and bade me come to-morrow.

Were I with her, the night would post too soon;
  But now are minutes added to the hours;
To spite me, now each minute seems a noon,
  Yet, not for me, shine sun to succour flowers.
Pack night, peep day, good day of night now borrow;
Short night, to-night, and length thyself to-morrow.

---

## CATCH.—Three Voices and Chorus.

*Webbe.*

Pray, good Sir, will you do us the favour
To join in a catch?—Sir, I'll do my endeavour:—
To be sure I've a cold,—but I'll still do my best;
As I know your intention, I'll join with the rest.
  May the smiles of the company thus ever cheer us,
  And we all give pleasure to those who may hear us.

## GLEE.—Five Voices.

SHAKESPEARE. *Stevens.*

Who is Sylvia? what is she?
   That all our swains commend her:
Holy, fair, and wise is she,
   The heav'n such grace did lend her,
That she might admir'd be.
Is she kind, as she is fair?
   For beauty lives with kindness:
Love doth to her eyes repair
   To help him of his blindness;
And being help'd, inhabits there.
Then to Sylvia, let us sing,
   That Sylvia is excelling;
She excels each mortal thing
   Upon the dull earth dwelling.
To her let us garlands bring;
She excels each mortal thing
Upon the dull earth dwelling.

---

## GLEE.—Four Voices.

*Spofforth.*

Health to my dear, and long unbroken years,
By storms unruffled, and unstain'd by tears:
Wing'd by new joys, may each white minute fly,
Spring on her cheek, and sunshine in her eye:
O'er that dear breast, where love and pity spring,
May peace eternal spread her downy wing;
Sweet beaming hope her path illumine still,
And fair ideas all her fancy fill.

### GLEE.—Five Voices.

BIRCH. *Attwood.*

In tattered weed, from town to town,
  Is hapless primrose doom'd to stray;
Compell'd a wretched wand'rer known,
  To seek a home from day to day;
    Barefoot as she strolls forlorn
    O'er the flint or pointed thorn,
    Silent must her sorrow be,
    Her madrigal, sweet charity.
At ev'ning will the village hind
  In rapture listen to her song,
And buy her toys, in hope to find
  What future joys to him belong.
            Barefoot, &c.

---

### GLEE.—Four Voices.

*Spofforth.*

Cease your music, gentle swains!
Saw ye Delia cross the plains?
Ev'ry thicket, ev'ry grove,
Have I ranged to find my love.
A kid, a lamb, my flock I'd give,
Tell me only doth she live?
White her skin as mountain snow,
In her cheek the roses blow,
And her eye, is brighter far
Than the beaming morning star.
Tell me, shepherds! have ye seen
My delight, my love, my queen?

### ELEGY.—Three Voices and Chorus.

*(In Memory of Alexander Earl of Eglington.)*

Dr. Boyce.

Genius of Harmony; thy numbers lend,
   To grace an Eglington's lamented name;
Patrons, and sons of music, here attend,
   And swell the strain that consecrates his fame.
Lost! e'er the half of life's short race he ran,
   By ruthless hands forc'd to the shades below:
Not all the charms, or real worth of man,
   Could guard their vo'try from the fatal blow.
How vain our tears! how faint th' applause we pay!
   Yet grateful still this trophy meet we raise,
Whose basis deep in harmony we lay,
   So sweet accords shall eternize his praise.

---

### GLEE.—Four Voices.

Dr. Callcott.

Oh sov'reign of the willing soul,
   Parent of sweet and solemn breathing airs;
   Enchanting shell! the sullen cares,
And frantic passions, hear thy soft controul.
On Thracia's hills, the Lord of War,
Has curb'd the fury of his car,
And dropt his thirsty lance at thy command:
Perching on the scept'red hand of Jove,
Thy magic lulls the feather'd king;
With ruffled plumes and flagging wing;
Quench'd in dark clouds of slumber lie,
The terror of his beak, and lightnings of his eye.

## THE SQUIRREL.
### GLEE.—Four Voices.

ROSCOE.                      Sir G. J. Smart.

I LOVE to see, at early morn,
   The squirrel sit before my door;
There crack his nuts, and hide his shells,
   And leap away to seek for more.
I love in hedge-row paths to see
   The linnet glance from spray to spray,
Or mark at ev'nings balmy close;
   The red-breast hop across my way:
For sure when Nature's free-born train,
   Approach with song and gambol near,
Some secret impulse bids them feel,
   The footsteps of a friend are there.

---

### GLEE.—Four Voices.

HORACE.                 Stevens. Medal, 1782.

SEE what horrid tempests rise,
And contract the clouded skies;
Snows and showers fill the air,
And bring down the atmosphere.
Hark what tempests sweep the floods!
How they shake the rattling woods!

Let us, while its in our power,
Let us seize the fleeting hour;
While our cheeks are fresh and gay,
Let us drive old age away.
Then let joy and mirth be thine,
Mirthful songs, and joyous wine,
And with converse blithe and gay,
Drive all gloomy cares away.

## 44

### GLEE.—Three Voices.
ANACREON.                                         *S. Wesley.*

WHEN Bacchus, Jove's immortal boy,
The rosy harbinger of joy;
Who, with the sunshine of the bowl,
Thaws the winter of our soul.
When to my inmost core he glides,
And bathes it with his ruby tides;
A flow of joy, a lively heat,
Fires my brain and wings my feet.
'Tis surely something sweet, I think,
Nay something heav'nly sweet to drink;
Sing, sing of love, let music's breath!
Soft beguile our rapturous death.
While my young Venus, thou, and I,
To the voluptuous cadence die;
Then, waking from our languid trance,
Again we'll sport, again we'll dance.

---

### GLEE.—Five Voices.
OSSIAN.                                            *Dr. Callcott.*

THOU art beautiful queen of the valley,
Thy walls like silver sparkle to the sun;
Melodious wave thy groves:
Thy garden sweets enrich the pleasant air;
Upon the lake lie the long shadows of thy towers,
And high in heaven thy temple pyramids arise.
Queen of the valley thou art beautiful:
Long! long may'st thou flourish in thy beauty.
Long prosper beneath the righteous conqueror
Who conquers to redeem:
Long years of peace await thy Lord, and thee,
Queen of the Valley.

## TO APOLLO.
### GLEE.—Four Voices and Chorus.

HORACE. *Stevens.*

When at Apollo's hallow'd shrine
The poet hails the pow'r divine,
What is the blessing he implores,
While he the first libation pours?
He not desires the swelling grain,
That yellows o'er Sardinia's plain;
Nor the fair herds that lowing feed
On warm Calabria's flow'ry mead;
Nor ivory of spotless shine,
Nor gold forth flaming from its mine.
To me boon nature frankly yields
Her richest vintage from the fields;
Nor ask I more than sense and health,
Still to enjoy my present wealth.
From age, and all its weakness free,
O son of Jove, preserv'd by thee,
Give me to strike the tuneful lyre,
And thou my latest song inspire.

---

### CANONE.—Three Voices.

*Cherubini.*

Perfida Clori
Tu m'ingannasti
E poi bramasti
Perfida Clori da me pieta.

## GLEE.—Four Voices.
MOORE.                    *Horsley, M. B.*

By Celia's arbour all the night,
   Hang humid wreath, the lover's vow;
And haply at the morning light,
   My love shall twine thee round her brow.
Then if upon her bosom bright,
   Some drops of dew shall fall from thee;
Tell her, they are not drops of night,
   But tears of sorrow shed by me.

---

## GLEE.—Four Voices.
                                     *Webbe.*

Hail, happy meeting! vintage now is done;
The grapes are purpled by th' autumnal sun,
Who having with his beams all nature blest,
Retires to Capricorn, and sinks to rest.
Now comes relentless Winter, that deforms
With frost the forest, and the sea with storms.
We shun the rage, and thus in social mirth
We'll pass our time, 'till Spring renews its birth.
Hail, happy meeting! crown'd with every blessing;
Thrice happy we, such plenty here possessing,
Each in his look his heart's content expressing.
Thus while together such a treat before us,
Since it hath pleas'd great Bacchus to restore us,
Cantet nunc Io Amicorum Chorus.

## SIGHS.
### GLEE.—Four Voices.

*Sir G. J. Smart.*

What are sighs? but sorrows breeze,
Blowing o'er life's ruffled seas:
What are we? barks sailing o'er
To a distant tranquil shore:
Pilots then unfurl the sail,
Quickly seize the fav'ring gale,
This will waft you to yon sphere,
Free from trouble, free from fear.
Breath of sadness, fill my soul,
Waft me to that distant goal;
Airy wing, come bear me home,
Upwards never more to roam;
Sigh, thou brother of a tear,
Freely welcome, freely here,
On thee, my soul would gladly rise
To its peaceful home the skies.

---

### GLEE.—Four Voices.

Shakespeare.     *Stevens.*

Crabbed age and youth cannot live together;
  Youth is full of pleasure, age is full of care;
Youth like summer morn, age like winter weather;
  Youth like summer brave, age like winter bare.

Age, I do abhor thee! youth, I do adore thee!
  O my love, my love is young:
Age, I do defy thee! Oh! sweet shepherd hie thee!
  For, methinks, thou stay'st too long.

## 48

### GLEE.—Five Voices.
*C. Smith.*

Spring returns with aspect mild,
Violet crown'd, her loveliest child;
Now again the ruddy thorn
Glitters with the dew of morn:
Buzzing round sweet cowslip bells,
Bees suck nectar from their cells;
The vivid flash from beauty's eye,
When tell-tale love is lurking nigh;
The pleading look, the starting tear,
That parting lovers often wear;
The balmy kiss, the gentle sigh,
Escaping, yet it knows not why:
All hail the lovely bloom of op'ning spring!
While Cupid's arrows flutter from its wing.

### GLEE.—Three Voices.
*Attwood.*

With heart and hand come let us join,
   Our cares behind us cast;
And love and friendship's wreath entwine,
   To bloom while life shall last:
The world may smile, the world may frown,
   Its blights and wintry blasts are rude;
Here Jack goes up, and Jill goes down,
   And man follows fortune's mood.
But he alone is fit on earth to live,
   Whose wants are the wants of another;
And bless'd is the man, who, blessing will give
   Half a loaf of his bread to his brother.
*Da Capo.*

## GLEE.—Four Voices.

Sir JOHN HARRINGTON.                 *Stevens.*

WHENCE comes my love? O heart! disclose:
'Twas from cheeks that sham'd the rose;
From lips that spoil the rubies' praise;
From eyes that mock the diamond's blaze.
Whence comes my woe? as freely own,
Ah me! 'twas from a heart like stone.

The blushing cheek speaks modest mind,
The lips befitting words most kind;
The eye doth tempt to Love's desire,
And seems to say, 'tis Cupid's fire;
Yet all so fair, but speak my moan,
Since nought doth say the heart of stone.

Why thus, my love, so kind, bespeak,
Sweet lip, sweet eye, sweet blushing cheek,
Yet not a heart to save my pain;
O Venus, take thy gifts again!
Make not so fair, to cause our moan,
Or make a heart that's like our own.

---

## MOTET.—Five Voices.

THOMSON.                 *Dr. Crotch.*

Hallelujah, Amen.

METHINKS I hear the full celestial choir,
   Through heaven's high dome their awful anthems raise;
Now chaunting clear, and now they all conspire
   To swell the lofty hymn from praise to praise.

### GLEE.—Four Voices.
*Sir George Smart.*

Queen of the skies, who silver'st wide
This dreary world with glory's sea,
Roll from thy orb the radiant tide,
And pour thy lucid streams on me.
Here muffled dark, in horror's dread,
I bow to sacred Love's command;
While anguish clasps my aching head,
And terror chills with palsied hand.
Oh hear! O guide these wilder'd feet
To where my lov'd Hedalleen stays;
Give me his long-lost form to meet,
To light his eyes with fond amaze.
Give him, oh! ere with life he part,
Give him to lull these wild alarms;
Once more to soothe his dying heart.
Once more to bless his Melna's arms.

---

### GLEE.—Four Voices and Chorus.
Congreve.                                                *Webbe.*

Thy voice, O Harmony! with awful sound,
Could penetrate th' abyss profound!
Explore the realms of ancient night,
And search the living source of unborn light:
Confusion heard thy voice and fled,
And Chaos deeper plung'd his vanquish'd head.
Then didst thou, Harmony, give birth
To this fair form of heaven and earth!
Then, all those shining worlds above,
In mystic dance began to move,
Around the radiant sphere of central fire,
A never ceasing, never silent choir!

## GLEE.—Four Voices.

Ossian. *Dr. Callcott.*

In the lonely vale of streams abides the narrow soul. Years roll on, seasons return, but he is still unknown.

In a blast comes cloudy death, and lays his grey head low. His ghost is folded in the vapour of the fenny field. Its course is never on hills, nor mossy vales of wind.

---

## GLEE.—Three Voices.
*(Occasioned by hearing Non Nobis ill sung.)*

*Dr. Harrington.*

What shall we sing; now here are three,
Let it be Non Nobis Domine;
Hold, Sir! indeed that's wrong.
I'm sure 'tis right, 'tis you that's wrong,
Begin again, it is not so, Sir;
You are both wrong—I'll sing no more to-night, Sir.

---

## CATCH.—Four Voices.

*Webbe.*

Would you know my Celia's charms,
Which now excite my fierce alarms?
I'm sure she's fortitude and truth,
To gain the heart of ev'ry youth.
She's only thirty lovers now;
The rest are gone, I can't tell how!
No longer Celia ought to strive,
For, certainly, she's—fifty-five!

## GLEE.—Four Voices.

*Spofforth.*

The spring, the pleasant spring is blown;
Let us leave the smoky town;
From the mall, and from the ring,
Ev'ry one has taken wing!
Chloe, Strephon, Corydon,
All are fled, and all are gone;
What is left's not worth your stay,
Come, Aurelia, come away!

Come, with all thy sweetest smiles,
With thy graces, with thy wiles;
Come, and we will merry be;
Who shall be so blest as we?
We will frolic all the day,
Harming no one in our play;
No matter what the people say;
Come, Aurelia, come away!

---

## GLEE.—Five Voices.

Horace, *Carmen* 30.  *Dr. Cooke.*

O Venus! Regina Cnidi, Paphique,
Sperne dilectam Cypron, & vocantis
Thure te multo Glyceræ decoram
    Transfer in ædem.
Fervidus tecum Puer, & solutis
Gratiæ zonis, properèntque Nymphæ
Et parùm comis sine te Juventas,
    Mercuriusque

### GLEE.—Three Voices and Chorus.
*(With a Double Accompaniment.)*

OSSIAN.                                                                Attwood.

Rise to the battle, my thousands; pour round me like the echoing main. Gather round the bright steel of your king. Strong as the rocks of my land, that meet the storm with joy. and stretch their dark woods to the wind.

---

### GLEE.—Five Voices.

MOORE.                                                              Attwood.

To all that breathe the air of heav'n,
Some boon of strength has Nature given:
When the majestic bull was born,
She fenc'd his brow with wreathed horn:
She arm'd the courser's foot of air,
And wing'd with speed the panting hare:
She gave the lion fangs of terror;
And, in the ocean's chystal mirror,
Taught the unnumber'd scaly throng
To trace the liquid path along:
While, for the umbrage of the grove,
She plum'd the warbling world of love.
To man, she gave the flame refin'd,
The spark of heav'n!—a thinking mind:
And had she no surpassing treasure
For thee, O woman! child of pleasure?
She gave thee beauty—shaft of eyes,
That ev'ry shaft of war outflies:
She gave thee beauty—blush of fire,
That bid the flames of war retire.
Woman, be fair! we must adore thee!
Smile! and a world is weak before thee.

## 54

GLEE.—Four Voices.

*Battishill.*

The glories of our birth and state,
  Are shadows, not substantial things:
There is no armour 'gainst our fate!
  Death lays his icy hands on kings!
    Sceptre and crown must tumble down,
  And in the dust be equal made
  With the poor crooked scythe and spade.

Some men with swords may reap the field,
  And plant fresh laurels where they kill:
But their strong nerves at last must yield,
  Subdued by one another still!
    Early or late they stoop to fate,
  And must give up their murm'ring breath,
  When they, pale captives, creep to death.

The garlands wither on your brow,
  Then boast no more your mighty deeds.
Upon Death's purple altar, now,
  See where the victor victim bleeds:
    All heads must come to the cold tomb.
  Only the actions of the just
  Smell sweet, and blossom in the dust.

---

REQUIEM.—Four Voices.

Miss Starke.  *Stevens.*

Saints and angels, hear our strains,
  From purging fire her soul convey,
And waft it to those blest domains,
  Where smiling joy feels no decay.

## GLEE.—Three Voices.

Sir JOHN MOORE, Bart. *Stevens.*

IF in that breast, so good, so pure,
　Compassion ever lov'd to dwell;
Pity the sorrows I endure,
　The cause I must not, dare not tell.

The grief, that on my quiet preys,
　That rends my heart, and checks my tongue,
I fear will last me all my days,
　But know it cannot last me long.

---

## GLEE.—Four Voices.

*Attwood.*

VIRTUE, my Emma, is a gem,
The mind's pellucid diadem;
To fellow mortals kindly given,
A foretaste and a type of Heaven!
Pure and white, as mountain snow
That hurries to the vale below;
Yet genial as the glorious sun
Which makes it unpolluted run.
Yet, as the mind disfigur'd grows,
Her careless course discolour'd flows:
So in the mind dark clouds arise,
And God's emanant gifts disguise.
But Virtue, that hath taken root,
Tears from the mind each wayward shoot;
And, like a stream thro' flow'ry meads,
Gives beauty to the bounds she feeds.

## WITCHES SONG AND CHORUS.—Five Voices.

BEN JONSON. *Stevens.*

### FIRST WITCH.

I have been all day looking after
A raven feeding upon a quarter;
And soon as she turn'd her beak to the south,
I snatch'd this morsel out of her mouth.

### FIFTH WITCH.

I last night lay all alone
O' the ground, to hear the mandrake groan;
And pluck'd him up, tho' he grew full low:
And, as I had done, the cock did crow.

### SECOND WITCH.

And I have been chusing out this skull
From charnel-houses that were full;
From private grots, and public pits;
And frighted a Sexton out of his wits.

### FIRST WITCH.

Under a cradle I did creep
By day; and when the child was asleep
At night, I suck'd the breath; and rose,
And pluck'd the nodding nurse by the nose.

### FOURTH WITCH.

A murderer, yonder, was hung in chains;
The sun and the wind had shrunk his veins:
I bit off a sinew; I clipp'd his hair;
I brought off his rags, that danc'd in the air.

CHORUS.

We have brought, to aid our vows,
Horned poppy, cypress boughs,
The fig tree wild, that grows on tombs,
And juice that from the larch tree comes,
  The basilisk's blood, the viper's skin:
  And now our orgies let's begin.

---

GLEE.—Four Voices.

WITHER, 1614.                        *Stevens*

Hence, away! ye Syrens leave me,
  And unclasp your wanton arms;
Sugar'd words can ne'er deceive me,
  Though you prove a thousand charms.
Fye, fye, forbear; no common snare
  Could ever my affection chain;
Your painted baits, and poor deceits,
  Are all bestow'd on me in vain.

Can he prize the tainted posies,
  Which on every breast are worn;
That may pluck the spotless roses
  From their never touched thorn?
I can rest on her sweet breast,
  That is the pride of Cynthia's train;
Then hold your tongues; your mermaid songs
  Are all bestow'd on me in vain.

## GLEE.—Five Voices.

Sir PHILIP SIDNEY. *Stevens.*

All my sense thy sweetness gained;
Thy dear hair my heart enchained:
My poor reason thy words moved,
So that thee like Heaven I loved.
    Fal lal leridan, dan dan deridan,
    Deridan, deridan, deridan, dei;
    Fal lal leridan, dan dan deridan,
    Deridan, deridan, deridan, dei,
    Deridan, deridan, deridan, dei.

Now thy sweetness sour is deemed;
Thy hair not worth a hair esteemed:
Reason hath thy words removed,
Finding that but words they proved.
    Fal lal leridan, &c.

Woe to me, alas! she weepeth!
Fool! in me what folly creepeth!
Was I to blaspheme enraged
Where my soul I have engaged.
    Fal lal leridan, &c.

Sweetness! sweetly pardon folly;
Tie me, hair, your captive wholly;
Words, O words, of heav'nly knowledge,
Know, my words their faults acknowledge.
    Fal lal leridan, &c.

## GLEE.—Four Voices.

SHENSTONE. *Stevens.*

Adieu, ye jovial youths, who join
To plunge old Care in floods of wine?
And, as your dazzled eye-balls roll,
Discern him struggling in the bowl.
Nor yet is hope so wholly flown,
Nor yet is thought so tedious grown,
But limpid stream and shady tree
Retain, as yet, some sweets for me.
And see, through yonder silent grove,
See yonder does my Daphne rove:
With pride her footsteps I pursue,
And bid your frantic joys adieu.
The sole confusion I admire
Is that my Daphne's eyes inspire:
I scorn the madness you approve,
And value reason next to love.

## GLEE.—Five Voices.

SHAKESPEARE. *Stevens.*

Orpheus with his lute made trees,
And the mountain tops that freeze,
   Bow themselves when he did sing.
To his music, plants and flowers
Ever sprung, as sun and showers
   There had made a lasting spring.

Ev'ry thing that heard him play,
Even the billows of the sea,
   Hung their heads, and then lay by.
In sweet music is such art,
Killing care and grief of heart,
   Fall asleep, or hearing, die.

## GLEE.—Four Voices.

WALLER.  Stevens.

Go, lovely rose!
Tell her that wastes her time, and me,
　That now she knows,
When I resemble her to thee,
How sweet, and fair, she seems to be.


Tell her that's young,
And shuns to have her graces spy'd,
　That hadst thou sprung
In deserts, where no men abide,
Thou must have uncommended dy'd.


Then die! that she
The common fate of all things rare
　May read in thee:
How small a part of time they share
That are so wond'rous sweet, and fair!

---

## GLEE.—Five Voices.

PIOZZI.  Stevens.

When lurking love, in ambush lies,
Under friendship's fair disguise;
When he wears an angry mien,
Imitating spite or spleen;
When like sorrow, he seduces;
When like pleasure, he amuses;
Still, howe'er the parts are cast,
'Tis but lurking love at last.

## FANCY AND DESIRE.
### GLEE.—Five Voices.

Earl of OXFORD, 1562. *Stevens.*

COME hither, shepherd's swain;
　"Sir, what do you require?"
I pray thee, shew to me thy name:
　"My name is fond Desire."

Tell me, who was thy nurse?
　"Fresh youth in sugar'd joy:"
What was thy meat and daily food?
　"Sad sighs with great annoy."

What lull'd thee then asleep?
　"Sweet speech, which likes me best."
Tell me, where is thy dwelling-place?
　"In gentle hearts I rest."

Doth either time or age
　Bring him unto decay?
"No, no: Desire both lives and dies
　Ten thousand times a day."

Then, fond Desire, farewell,
　Thou art no mate for me;
I should be loth, methinks, to dwell
　With such a one as thee.

## GLEE.—Four Voices.

*Stevens.*

Over the mountains,
 And over the waves;
Under the fountains,
 And under the graves;
Over floods that are deepest,
 Which Neptune obey;
Over rocks that are steepest,
 Love will find out the way.

Where there is no place
 For the glow-worm to lye;
Where there is no space
 For receipt of a fly;
Where the midge to venture dares not,
 Lest fast herself she lay;
If Love come, why he cares not,
 But soon finds out the way.

Some think to lose him,
 By having him confin'd;
And some do suppose him,
 Poor thing, to be blind;
But if ne'er so close ye wall him,
 Do the best that you may,
Blind Love, if so you call him,
 Will find out the way.

You may esteem him
  A child for his might;
Or you may deem him
  A coward from his flight;
But if she, whom love doth honour,
  Be conceal'd from the day,
Set a thousand guards upon her,
  Love will find out the way.

You may train the eagle
  To stoop to your fist;
Or you may inveigle
  The phœnix of the east;
The lioness, ye may move her
  To give o'er her prey;
Yet will you ne'er discover
  When Love finds out the way.

### SICILIAN MARINER'S HYMN.—Five Voices.

O sanctissima, O piissima,
Dulcis Virgo Maria,
  Mater amata,
  Intemerata,
  Ora pro nobis.

### GLEE.—Four Voices.

SHAKESPEARE. *Stevens.*

Doubt thou the stars are fire,
Doubt thou the sun doth move,
Doubt truth to be a liar,
But never doubt I love.

## 64

GLEE.—Three Voices.

SHAKESPEARE. *King.*

When shall we three meet again,
In thunder, lightning, or in rain?
When the hurly-burly's done,
When the battle's lost and won,
That will be ere set of sun.

---

GLEE.—Four Voices.

SHAKESPEARE. *Stevens.*

Now the hungry lion roars,
  And howling wolves behold the moon;
While the heavy ploughman snores,
  All with weary task foredone.
Now the wasted brands do glow,
  While the screech-owl, screeching loud,
Puts the wretch, that lies in woe,
  In remembrance of a shroud.
Now it is the time of night,
  When the graves all gaping wide,
Ev'ry one lets forth his sprite,
  In the church-way path to glide.
And we fairies that do run;
  By the triple Hecate's team,
From the presence of the sun,
  Follow darkness as a dream.

www.ingramcontent.com/pod-product-compliance
Lightning Source LLC
Chambersburg PA
CBHW020237170426
43202CB00008B/119